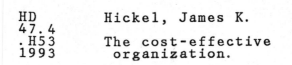

DATE			

BAKER & TAYLOR

THE
COST-EFFECTIVE
ORGANIZATION

THE
COST-EFFECTIVE
ORGANIZATION

How to Create It
How to Maintain It

James K. Hickel

Glenbridge Publishing Ltd.

Library of Congress Catalog Card Number: 93-77879

International Standard Book Number: 0-944435-22-X

To Joanne, Alanna, and Amelia

Contents

Acknowledgments

A few paragraphs in this book were taken from the following previously published articles:

"Restructuring? Avoid the Myths," *Communications World,* April 1989 (with Joel H. Head, currently Regional Director of the Communications Practice for Ernst and Young)

"What Happens After Restructuring?" *Journal of Business Strategy,* July/August 1990, copyright © Faulkner & Gray Inc. (with David H. Ulm, currently President of Quality Management Reporting Systems)

Thanks to both publications, and both of my co-authors of these articles, for their permission to use some of that material here.

My thanks also go to each and every one of my clients over the past fifteen years. I hope they've learned as much from me as I've learned from them.

Introduction

Cost Reduction vs. Cost Control

> Cost reduction is like going on a diet. Cost control is like staying in shape. Many have dieted successfully, but how many have managed to keep the weight off?

Economists often talk about the "business cycle." It's the cyclical nature of the economy that causes our modern business environment to "boom-and-bust." Each period of good times and free spending, it seems, is quickly followed by a recession, layoffs, and an uncomfortable tightening of belts.

Several factors go into the making of a business cycle. One of the most important is human nature. When times are good, there is a tendency to overspend. When times are

1

lean, there is a tendency to pull back. This is as true for corporations as it is for individuals.

The "boom-and-bust" cycle has affected individual companies in strange ways. Some companies have a historical pattern of dramatically reducing the number of employees during recessions. Morale and productivity drag as the remaining employees struggle to keep up with the workload. When the recession ends and the boom period hits, the companies—hard hit from overwork that results when staffs are arbitrarily reduced and backlogged with customer demands—overhire to reduce the backlog and to provide a much-needed break for their personnel. Then, they wind up with more employees than they had before the last recession started! When the next recession hits, the companies have even more fat to trim from the payroll. This pattern may continue until the situation resembles, in the words of one nuclear engineer, "a sine wave that can quickly go critical."

In other words, the effect of these cycles on the quality and timeliness of the work soon becomes intolerable to managers, employees—and most important, to customers.

Much has been written, spoken, and done about *cost reduction* in past recessions by businesses worldwide. Those techniques are spelled out in Part One of this book, and the activities performed by any organization should be frequently checked against the milestones and measures that are inherent in those mechanisms.

Surprisingly, however, little has been done about *cost control*—the techniques spelled out in Part Two, techniques that help avoid the need for painful and difficult cost and employee reductions in the future. Will organizations remain streamlined and competitive during the next boom cycle? Or will it be business as usual, with excited hordes of management consultants and outplacement specialists eagerly awaiting the workload that will result from the next economic downturn? The choice is yours.

There are remarkable similarities between cost reduction and cost control. Both involve similar steps: guiding and managing the organization in a consistent direction, and setting up clear mechanisms for measuring the cost of the services being performed both by and for the organization.

But there are principles that underlie both cost reduction and cost control and are critically important to both.

> Cost reduction and cost control both require the active participation and support of senior management.

Senior management is always a critical factor in setting priorities for an organization. Several years ago at one Virginia-based corporation, the chairman of the board was nearly a half-hour late for his regular morning senior staff meeting. Red-faced, he fumed to his collected officers, "It took me twenty minutes to drive around the block and get into the building. Why don't we have an entrance to the garage on the Main Street side of our building?" He then began the meeting and gradually cooled down, completely forgetting about the incident by the end of the day.

The next morning, the chairman drove to the office, only to discover that workers with jackhammers were opening up an entrance to the garage on the Main Street side. "Isn't that a coincidence?" the chairman thought. "I just mentioned this to my vice presidents yesterday. . . ."

Reality suddenly hit home, and when he arrived at his office, he questioned some of his officers. Sure enough, one of the chairman's employees took his casual remark as gospel and ordered the Building Services Department to open up another garage entrance for "His Highness."

When someone with the title of Chairman, President or Chief Executive Officer speaks, the rest of the organization listens. When senior management interest in cost-effectiveness is high, the entire organization concentrates on identifying opportunities to reduce cost—reluctantly at first, and then with more and more enthusiasm as employees recognize that cost control is rewarded and approved. On the other hand, when senior management interest in cost-effectiveness dwindles, as it often can, particularly when the market and the economy are good, the organizational effort devoted to cost-effectiveness also declines.

Senior management participation in cost-reduction and cost-control efforts must be active, visible, and continuous. It cannot be delegated. So many time-honored precedents must be reversed in the process of achieving cost-effectiveness that it cannot be implemented without the active backing of the person at the top.

> Cost reduction and cost control are revolutionary concepts. They are heretical and counterintuitive in modern business, and therefore must be patiently taught and continually reinforced.

Modern business tends to reward power and authority, defined as both the ability to order other people around and the ability to spend money. Not only does the psychology of the modern business organization equate power and authority with self-esteem, but the compensation paid by the organization is frequently directly related to the power and authority exercised by its employees. The more money you spend and the more people you have reporting to you, the more money you make.

The cost-effective organization reverses these long-held and cherished tenets of modern business management. The cost-effective organization:

- Rewards employees for reducing the number of people in their department—and, yes, even eliminating their department entirely

- Rewards those who continuously work to reduce their costs, and punishes those who engage in last-minute spending sprees to use up their budgets before the end of the fiscal year

- Rewards those who keep few organizational levels between themselves and their employees, and punishes those who build a massive organizational pyramid to keep themselves aloof from the proletariat

- Renounces a business management philosophy that virtually ensures each employee a job for life, and adopts a philosophy that requires each employee to periodically justify his or her value to the organization

Please don't misunderstand. Small is not necessarily beautiful. The purpose of cost reduction and cost control is to make you and your company rich. And part of that process, in the current business climate, is providing high-quality service at a rock-bottom price.

In the final analysis, cost-effectiveness means providing the highest customer satisfaction at the lowest possible cost. And that translates into higher pay and greater job satisfaction for all of us.

> Cost control is better than cost reduction.

In a major emergency, of course, you may have no choice but to undertake an organization-wide cost-reduction effort. And many successful companies have had to do precisely that when the economy has turned down.

But when the competition is gnawing at your heels and the income statement looks grim, it's a particularly difficult time to step back and take a long hard look at the way the company does business. And the effect on morale that results when employees are laid off in order to meet cost-reduction goals can be devastating.

Typically, the order of preference is:

- *Ongoing cost control,* which should be done by all departments within the organization on a continuous basis. This allows the organization to judiciously "prune" costs and to maintain maximum profitability.

- *Selective cost reduction,* which should be performed for a particular department or set of departments, when those departments operate at cost levels that do not appear to be fully justified or are not matched by the competition.

- *Organizational cost reduction,* which involves a review of all functions performed throughout the organization. Organizational cost reduction should be performed when reasonable economic data indicate that competitor prices have had or will have a significant negative impact on your market share, that the difference between your costs and your competitor's contributes to that impact, and when those cost differences cannot readily be isolated to a clearly identifiable set of functions or departments.

If you can maintain or improve your competitiveness simply by utilizing cost-control mechanisms, do it. But if there are pockets of severe inefficiency within your organization, or if costs overall are so out of line that your market share is rapidly declining, there is no substitute for an all-out cost-reduction effort.

Part One
Cost Reduction

1
Cost Reduction

You can reduce costs by canceling a million dollar
capital project, by buying fewer paper clips, or both.
The right way to reduce costs is different for each
company.

For one company's major cost-reduction effort, we set
up two teams, each consisting of five company managers.
Each team, guided by a consultant, examined ways for
the company to reduce costs and save money. One team
was known as the Technical Team, because it examined
technical areas such as manufacturing and operations.
The other team was the Administrative Team, and looked
at administrative areas such as human resources and public relations.

The Technical Team quickly came up with a recommendation that the company should shut down its major manufacturing plant, saving the company $20 million a year. Satisfied with the big dollars associated with their idea, the Technical Team looked down its nose at its colleagues on the Administrative Team who came up with smaller-scale recommendations, such as "quit sending out acknowledgment letters to unsolicited résumés," and "don't send more than one public relations person to community meetings." Whenever the Technical Team members passed the work area of the Administrative Team, they would pick up a few of the Administrative Team's work papers, examine the recommendations with disdain, and sniff, "nickel and dime stuff."

Meanwhile, the Technical Team concentrated almost all of its efforts on solidifying its $20 million a year plant shutdown recommendation.

When it came time to present the preliminary recommendations to senior management, the Administrative Team had about a hundred recommendations that added up to a substantial cost savings. Although senior management fine tuned those recommendations and even eliminated or substantially altered a recommendation or two, most of the recommendations were implemented successfully.

On the other hand, the shutdown of a major manufacturing plant generated several hours of debate among senior managers and board members who ultimately decided against the recommendation. With few other recommendations in their portfolio, the Technical Team scrambled to develop cost-reduction recommendations that would match the impact projected for the Administrative Team.

And while they scrambled, the Administrative Team chortled, "nickel and dime, nickel and dime."

In the words of one business manager who is fond of hunting, "If you want a lot of meat, you can either shoot one elephant or a lot of jack rabbits. Your hunting strategy depends largely on whether you are in Africa or Nebraska."

Similarly, the spending patterns of your organization may require that you concentrate on a single cost-reduction opportunity, or that you identify hundreds of smaller spending items. In most cases, the successful cost-reduction effort results in both types of opportunities.

Before we examine what cost reduction is, however, it is important to examine what it is not.

> Across-the-board reductions and arbitrary top-down edicts to reduce costs don't work.

You've seen it in all types of organizations everywhere, innumerable times. "We've got to get our costs down," the boss decrees. "We're going to reduce each department's budget by ten percent."

It's a popular and relatively easy cost-reduction mechanism. The across-the-board reduction is particularly popular in governmental organizations because it helps avoid making political choices and offending interest groups. But the beneficial aspects of such across-the-board decrees tend to be short-term while the damaging aspects linger:

- Busy departments cut back on doing all types of necessary work, putting it on the back burner for later. When "later" comes and the budget is no longer so tight, the department not only hires back all the positions that it left unfilled during the crunch, but it sometimes needs even more people to reduce the backlog of work that was created when there weren't enough employees.

- Perhaps even worse, the organization has punished the responsible managers who have kept their expenses to a minimum, while rewarding those managers who kept secret pockets of fat in their budgets. The responsible, cost-conscious managers are forced to scrimp even further to come up with their ten-percent reduction, while the managers with fattened budgets simply skim off a little of their fat. The lesson learned by all managers for the future: Pad your budgets with unnecessary expenses that can be easily cut during the next cost crunch.

This phenomenon is true even with relatively minor cost-reduction efforts. At one large trade association that had suffered a temporary drop in revenues, the president of the association ordered an across-the-board ten-percent reduction in travel costs. The short-term impact was positive, as the amount of travel and its associated costs were substantially reduced. As the revenue picked up and the crisis eased, however, some travel budgets increased to levels ten to fifteen percent above the pre-crisis amount.

As it turned out, when times improved again, some managers were taking unnecessary or preventable trips in order to have enough travel expense built into their budgets to withstand the next cost-reduction edict.

Cost reduction requires a clear understanding of its impact on the organization. That means recognizing and communicating to employees and customers what work will no longer be performed and ensuring that the old work does not come quietly creeping back into the organization when times get better.

> Don't let your consultant drive the cost-reduction process.

Companies often hire outside consultants to help them with their downsizing or cost-reduction efforts, and then turn the reins over to those consultants, allowing them to make key management decisions. After the project is over, the consultant leaves, and the company is left with the consequences. Company management should run the company, not the consultant.

Most firms that engage in a major cost-reduction effort hire consultants to help with what can be a strange and complex process. But most cost-reduction activities, particularly those that lead to a major restructuring of a department or organization, are initially unpopular. It is tempting to let the outside consultant become the visible purveyor of the project, communicating—and taking the heat for— unwelcome decisions.

Employees, however, may find the restructuring harder to accept if it appears to be designed by outsiders. And the presence of a convenient scapegoat may lead some managers to develop a negative attitude toward the restructuring as well. Rejection of the cost-reduction effort by both management and employees can sometimes result in companies backing down from controversial cost-reduction ideas that might have been highly beneficial to the organization.

The most successful cost-reduction programs have involved complete and full participation of virtually all employees. This has included (1) full and active participation by the chief executive officer and other officers, (2) involvement of company employees as team members to conduct analyses and generate recommendations, (3) written surveys of all employees to solicit their ideas for cost reduction, (4) follow-up interviews with a large sample of selected employees, (5) meetings with groups of employees to discuss the cost-reduction process, and (6) where applicable, regular interaction with union representatives to discuss progress and possible alternatives.

Outside assistance may well be of value in your efforts to reduce costs, providing guidance and the benefit of experience with other companies. But, to be fully effective, the project should be clearly perceived by employees as the company's idea, conducted largely by company personnel with input from company employees. And the company should accept full responsibility for the implementation and ultimate success of the cost-reduction plan.

> On the other hand, cost-reduction projects should not be driven entirely by the desires of your managers and employees.

Although your employees should be the primary drivers behind the development of a cost-reduction plan, a certain amount of objectivity is required. Otherwise, the sacred cows will continue to graze on your corporate grassland.

When employees look for cost-reduction opportunities, they will naturally assess the political climate that surrounds their ideas. "Oh, we can't make that recommendation," they'll often say. "The president (or chairman, or vice president, or my boss) will never go for it."

A small electric utility in the Midwest routinely gave free light bulbs to all of its customers. Every few months, each customer was entitled to three free light bulbs. Such giveaways were common in the early days of electricity, when the local utility had to supply potential customers with light bulbs in order to develop the market for its product. Like many activities performed by older corporations, the light bulb giveaway was simply a program that had outlived its usefulness.

But when we proposed eliminating the light bulb giveaway, a chorus of objections arose from many company employees. "We can't make that recommendation," they said. "The light bulb program is too popular with customers." A review of customer survey data indicated, however, that most customers didn't take advantage of the light bulb program, and those who did raised little objection to its elimination, particularly if eliminating the program would help reduce the cost of electricity in their area.

"Well, we still can't make that recommendation," the naysayers continued, "because the board of directors has already rejected that idea." It was true that the board had voted against the idea of eliminating the giveaway, but that was six years ago. The new board, while still defensive of the program, was much more open to its elimination—particularly in light of the declining revenues of the utility and the pressing need to reduce costs.

Be it a consultant, customer representative, or outside board member, it helps to have a third party participate in the review to ensure that all of the sacred cows are being appropriately slaughtered.

> Comparing staffing levels at your company to the staffing levels at other companies is often an exercise in frustration.

A popular option for examining cost-reduction opportunities is to compare your company's staffing to the staffing levels of similar companies. For example, assume that Company A has ten attorneys in its legal department. The president of Company A discovers that Companies B, C, and D each have only five lawyers on their staff. Therefore, the president of Company A instructs the chief counsel to get rid of what the president believes to be five unnecessary employees.

However, no two companies are the same. The differences in staffing for our hypothetical legal departments could be that:

- Company A is going through some massive legal procedures or litigation that do not face Companies B, C, and D—and thus requires additional lawyers.

- Company B relies heavily on its outside law firm, spending three times as much on contracted legal services as Company A.

- Company C's legal staff is greatly overworked, and its General Counsel is about to request five more legal positions.

- Company D has lawyers scattered in departments throughout the company—Human Resources has its own attorney, as do the Finance, Engineering, and Construction departments—and these "satellite" lawyers weren't counted in the number given to Company A's president.

Looking at what other companies do and how they staff is important, but only as a preliminary guide for determining which areas of your company should be carefully scrutinized. But direct comparisons in and of themselves are often meaningless and should not be the sole or even primary basis for any type of resource reduction.

> There is only one way to successfully and permanently reduce costs: Through a rigorous analysis of all the functions performed throughout the organization.

Successful cost-reduction programs encompass all kinds of ideas and suggestions. Cost-reduction programs that have reduced costs by as much as 20 percent at some large organizations have involved:

- "Big" recommendations, such as eliminating entire divisions and sales offices and canceling major building programs

- "Moderate" recommendations, such as eliminating smaller units or buying material in bulk to obtain quantity discounts

- "Little" recommendations, such as replacing regular interoffice courier services with fax machines or streamlining the approval process for procurement and requisitions.

A mix of these types of recommendations has led to reductions of nearly $100 million per year at some organizations.

The key to such cost-cutting performances is the active involvement of as many company employees as possible. Employees should be charged with identifying and eliminating activities that will result in a reduced cost for the organization. In most organizations, even those that are reasonably well run, properly motivated employees can develop a surprising number of effective cost-reduction ideas.

All employees can be surveyed for their cost-reduction ideas. In addition, the best and most widely-respected employees can serve as full-time members of a team charged with identifying and developing major cost-reduction opportunities.

Employees should be encouraged to look outside their own familiar areas. For example, the engineering function should not be looked at by engineers alone but by engineers, accountants, lawyers, and everyone else in the organization—particularly those who are users of the function being performed. Give your best employees free rein, within a limited time period, to ask questions and conduct interviews within the organization, perhaps survey the employees, review internal documents, and talk to outsiders. Not only will this provide you with the best thinking your company has to offer, but it will give your best people the opportunity to learn about other areas of the company.

And, of course, there should be absolutely no recriminations for the team members who may suggest unpopular or unconventional methods of cost reduction.

> Rigorous analysis and identification of cost-reduction opportunities are performed by addressing several questions: What do we do? Why do we do it? How do we do it? How much do we pay for it? And who does it?

There are several analytical techniques that your company can apply to identify and develop cost-reduction opportunities. In summary, they are:

- *Functional Analysis ("What do we do?")*, which identifies the activities performed by the organization and where in the organization those activities are performed

- *Requirements Analysis ("Why do we do it?")*, which examines whether the underlying reason or requirement for each activity is valid in light of the organization's mission, goals, and objectives

- *Reengineering ("How do we do it?")*, which examines whether improvements can be made in the procedures used to perform the activity

- *Cost Analysis ("How much do we pay for it?")*, which identifies lower-cost alternatives for performing necessary activities

- *Organizational Analysis ("Who does it?")*, which examines the organization chart to determine whether there are opportunities for streamlining the structure.

These analytical techniques provide the foundation for building a cost-effective organization.

Approach to Cost Reduction

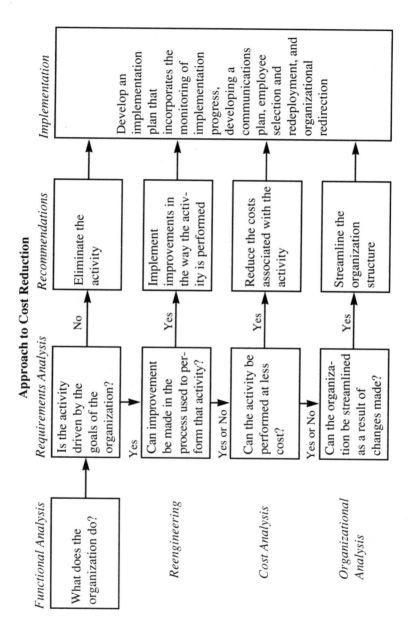

2
What Do We Do?
(Functional Analysis)

Finding out what your organization does is the most
important step in your cost-reduction effort. And it's
often the hardest.

"Your data is in error," the accounting manager for a
large company once told us. He was looking at the analysis
of functions that we performed for his organization. "Your
analysis shows that our accounting department is performing two man-years worth of engineering work. That's ridicu-
lous. We don't do any engineering work in our accounting
department."

Naturally, we went back to review the data and to talk
to the people who had provided that information. As it

turned out, the accounting department temporarily included several engineers who had been transferred over to do the financial analysis for a large capital project. Although those engineers were supposed to be concentrating on their accounting work, they tended to "sneak" engineering projects in on the side, both because their old boss from engineering asked them to do the work, and because they liked the familiar environment of engineering rather than the strange new world of accounting.

"Gee, I didn't know that," the accounting manager replied when he found out the data had been verified. "Better get those guys to concentrate on their accounting work a little more."

Either that, or get the company to recognize that more engineering work is going on than they realize.

What if the accounting manager had gone on blissfully unaware of the engineering services being performed by his department? In a cost-reduction atmosphere, several things could result—all of them bad:

- The company could decide that the accounting department is overstaffed for the amount of work that it puts out (not realizing that the equivalent of two accounting employees are not doing any accounting work at all) and could cut back the accounting department, thereby further stretching the resources of that department.

- The company could also decide that the engineering department is woefully understaffed for the large amount of work it puts out (not realizing that some of that work is performed by the accounting department), and thus add unnecessary engineers to the organization.

- If sufficiently stretched, the accounting department will ultimately ask for replacements for the missing employees. Human nature being what it is, the engineering department will not be as likely to call immediate attention to the fact that it is overstaffed.

- Perhaps worst of all, when word spreads throughout the company of this phenomenon (as word almost always does), cooperation among departments will be cut back substantially to avoid a similar result for other managers.

The experience of that accounting manager has been repeated dozens of times in companies that have attempted comprehensive cost-reduction programs. Finding out what your organization does isn't as easy as it sounds.

Reviewing the job descriptions doesn't always provide accurate information. Job descriptions tend to be somewhat ancient documents that were written to inflate the importance and compensation of the person in the position, rather than to describe the actual job performed.

Time sheets don't really do the job either. Although time sheets can play an important role for budgeting, project tracking, or regulatory purposes, they don't always accurately describe the specific job being performed. Besides, time sheets sometimes are filled out to meet the expectations of supervisors rather than to reflect actual work done.

The fact is there is rarely a single data base that provides sufficient detail on the work that is performed by any organization. To get that information, you have to go directly to the source.

> Finding out what your organization does involves the simple-sounding but intensive effort of asking people what they do.

There are two primary methods for asking people what their jobs are and what they do: Interviews (asking them in person) and surveys (asking them to write it down for you).

Through interviews, you ask people what they do for the organization. This process can save time and effort because often you can interview managers to find out what their subordinates do. The drawback is that, as illustrated with the story about the accounting manager, company executives aren't always fully aware of how their employees are actually employed.

Through surveys, you can ask precise questions of employees about what they do. The employees can provide estimates of time spent on each activity, and often—through a software program such as Lotus 1-2-3 or dBase III—you can print out reams of reports, detailing exactly what kinds of functions are performed by which departments or employees.

Surveys have the added advantage of allowing large groups of employees to participate in the process. Broad-based participation by most (or hopefully all) of the employees will create more popular acceptance of the usually unpopular recommendations that result from this kind of cost-reduction study.

While interviewing or surveying employees, you can ask questions of opinion such as: Where would you look for cost-reduction opportunities if you were performing this study? Or, how should cost-reduction ideas be implemented? This allows everyone to have a voice in the results of your cost-reduction effort.

While the degree of happiness with the recommendations—particularly recommendations that call for work-force reductions and organizational streamlining—is generally minimal, companies that actively involve as many employees as possible in the cost-reduction effort tend to be more successful in implementing the recommendations and realizing the savings that emerge from that effort.

Reviewing the budget will provide you with additional information about the functions that the company is performing and some that you may have forgotten about!

If you look simply at the functions that are being performed by employees within the company, you may be ignoring a substantial part of the company's operation.

Look for budget items that may not show up in a review of internal employee functions; some items include:

- Expenses for outside contractors

- Trade association dues and professional memberships

- Travel expenses

Each of these present opportunities for cost reduction, if examined using the same criteria applied to internal company functions. The company's budget may be the single most important internal document in a cost-reduction review.

It's easy to neglect some of the organization's activities and expenses without a budget review of this type. At one company, the employees conducted an extensive "activity-based" review of the company, focusing entirely at the functions that the company itself performed in order to reduce costs. Toward the end of the project, one of the vice presidents asked: "Have you looked at our advertising budget? It looks awfully high to me?" This activity was neglected because it was performed largely outside of the company, yet accounted for $15 million of the company expenses. The company employees hastily performed an analysis and determined that the advertising budget could be reduced significantly without affecting the company's success in the marketplace.

> There are gold nuggets to be mined from a comprehensive review of other internal documents.

Most companies have a number of additional documents that are routinely generated and can provide important information regarding cost-reduction opportunities. Some examples are:

Data Item	Analysis
Management letters from outside auditors	What kinds of issues have been identified in the management letters that the auditors provide? (Internal auditors routinely provide such letters, which informally inform management of possible problems, challenges

or opportunities in the way the company does business). Would these issues, if addressed, result in cost savings? Have all the issues identified by those auditors been addressed?

Securities and Exchange Commission (SEC) Form10K

What problems have been identified by the company in its 10K report to the Securities and Exchange Commission? (The 10K is a disclosure report that provides certain fundamental information to stockholders and potential stockholders.) Do these problems result in excessive costs? Are those problems being addressed?

Budget vs. actual variance reports

Are these reports clear and understandable to senior management? (These are the reports, usually monthly, that are circulated internally to explain to managers how well each department or unit is performing relative to the budget.)

Which items are "out of control," relative to the initial budgets developed? Are these expense variations adequately explained, and are steps being taken to control those costs?

Long-range capital/ construction expenditure forecasts	What impact will these projected expenses have on the resource requirements of the organization?
Contracts with suppliers	How have suppliers been selected? Is it a competitive bid process? If not, why not?

What recourse does the company have, contractually, in the event of a major upswing in prices? Can it get out of the contract, or minimize the volume of purchases required under the contract? If not, why not?

What recourse does the company have, contractually, in the event of a major downswing in prices? Is it required to purchase a large quantity of the product at a higher contractual price? If so, why?

What is the optimum low-cost supply strategy given the organization's demand projections? How does that optimum strategy differ, if at all, with the strategy currently in place? What steps could be taken to implement that optimum strategy?

Outside Consultants' Reports

What problems or issues were uncovered in previous consultant reports? What recommendations were made? Which recommendations are being implemented, and which are not? Why?

Marketing Forecasts

Is the company's marketing forecast well-coordinated with its construction/capital project forecast? (If the company projects an upward trend in construction or capital project requirements, while the projection of demand for its product remains flat or declines, the expense devoted to construction or capital projects may be able to be reduced.)

Absenteeism/Turnover statistics

Are there areas of the company where absenteeism or turnover is excessive? In those areas, could improved control of absenteeism improve productivity?

Facilities and number of employees

Are the number of employees, sales offices, or other facilities scattered throughout the marketing territory consistent with the number, location, and requirements of customers?

Mission statements for departments

Is there apparent overlap or duplication in the mission statements of the various departments?

Position descriptions for employees

Is there apparent overlap or duplication in the position descriptions of various employees?

Any other documents that your organization develops can be sources of valuable information on the functions that your company performs and the opportunities that exist to improve those functions.

> Developing an understanding of company activities is an important first step for the rest of your cost-reduction effort.

Unfortunately, functional analysis doesn't answer any questions. It only raises them. Once you've attained responses from everyone you've examined and have carefully reviewed your organization's budget and internal documents, however, you are ready to put that information together and to begin to examine which activities may be redundant or unnecessary.

3
Who Are We Doing This For?
(Requirements Analysis)

> If you're not serving the customer, you'd better be serving someone who is.

In the operations department of a large midwestern company, two employees devoted themselves almost full time to preparing and distributing what appeared to be an unnecessary monthly report. The employees who prepared the report insisted that the president of the company examined their report in detail and relied on it heavily.

However, when we asked the president about their report, he pointed to the most recent copy sitting in his trash can and grunted, "I never look at that thing."

Naturally, we were eager to return to the operating department employees to find out why they thought their report was so important to the company's president. One of the employees confidently reached back into a dusty set of files, pulled out a memo and exclaimed, "Here's your proof!" And sure enough, the memo emphasized the importance of the report, instructed that it be prepared monthly and widely distributed—and was signed by the president of the company.

Unfortunately, the memo was dated 1969. And the president who had signed it had long since retired and passed on.

Let's face it: As a general rule, dead presidents should not be running your company.

Finding out why your company does what it does (often called "requirements analysis") is a critical component of any cost-reduction effort.

Requirements analysis addresses the question, "Why is this work being performed?" It is the first step in determining whether there is an opportunity to reduce costs by cutting back or eliminating work performed by your company.

Suppose, for example, that your organization publishes a report that is distributed, on a monthly basis, to all employees. As you discuss this issue with company employees and managers, they may give you several different reasons why this report is being produced (with varying degrees of candor). Those reasons might include:

- "The report contains information necessary for the day-to-day operation of the business, such as budget information, sales data, or responses to customer satisfaction surveys."

- "The employee who prepares and distributes the report is a personal friend of a member of the board of directors, and the president feels that the employee has to be given some kind of a job to do."

- "The report facilitates communication among employees and departments, thereby encouraging team building and consensus within the company."

- "The report has been prepared and distributed for the past twenty years, and no one has ever complained about it or publicly argued that it was unnecessary."

- "By state law, the report must be approved and signed by the president of the company who wants to make sure that all company employees have an opportunity to review and comment first."

Each of these is a "requirement"; that is, it drives and motivates the work that is involved in preparing and distributing that report. Having identified all of the requirements for a given activity, the next step is to determine whether the underlying requirement is valid.

> The organization's strategic or business plan serves as a guide to the validity of the work it performs.

Your company's strategic plan should spell out, in broad terms, what guides and motivates the organization. If, by performing an activity, your organization moves closer to the goals and objectives spelled out in its plan, then that activity is said to have a valid underlying requirement.

Many companies with well-defined and effective planning processes also have mechanisms in place to ensure that all of the activities carried out by the organization, and all of the dollars spent by the organization, help to further its overall goals and objectives. Where this mechanism is fully developed and regularly monitored and enforced, requirements analysis may contribute little to the cost-reduction effort.

However, many companies do not have such mechanisms in place, and unnecessary activities may result. More than one company has made a conscious decision not to emphasize some area such as information systems or public relations in its strategic plan, considering such expenditures a waste of money. And more than one company manager has privately countermanded that decision by dedicating a considerable amount of money to those functions anyway, essentially ignoring the strategic plan because the manager disagrees with it. There may be literally thousands of companies throughout the country with "bootleg" information systems departments throughout the company, because managers who work there feel that insufficient resources are devoted to that area through the normal planning and budgeting process.

Still other companies can get into lines of business of which they are not even aware. One large manufacturing company had a rather entrepreneurial and aggressive manager as head of its print shop. "It drives me crazy to sit around managing one print order after another," the manager told us. "I need to make a bigger contribution to the company than that."

In order to increase company revenues, and to fit the needs of his hyperactive personality, the manager did subcontract printing and graphics work, using the printing plant during off-hours, with the approval of company management and contributing the profits directly to the company's bottom line. The business boomed, but the print shop manager began concentrating more on this outside business and less on the immediate need for printing services by the company itself. Eventually, the manager applied for more equipment and personnel to meet the demand of outside customers, and the company had to decide whether it was in the business of providing printing and graphic services. If so, the company would have to devote a large amount of new resources to the print shop, and if not, the print shop would have to be downscaled to merely meet the needs of the corporation.

The company's management came through with a clever and cost-effective solution: It decided, through its planning process, that it did not want to be in the business of providing printing and graphics support to other companies. It then sold the assets of its print shop to its print shop manager, who resigned from the company and continued to build the business independently while providing services to the company on a contracted basis. Printing became cheaper for the company, and the print shop manager was able to fully indulge his entrepreneurial skills.

A well-managed mechanism for monitoring company activities against the strategic plan can prevent unplanned activities from growing. Few companies have such mechanisms in place, however. In fact, a surprising number of companies have no formal strategic planning process at all.

Where there is no strategic plan, or if the plan does not set out clear objectives and goals for a given function, it is difficult to assess whether a requirement behind an activity is valid. In those situations, you need to make assumptions regarding the validity of a requirement. For most organizations, it is usually safe to assume that a strong underlying goal for the company is customer service and satisfaction.

> If there is no good strategic plan in place, then the customer should serve as the sole legitimate reason for performing all activities.

In the absence of a strategic plan or mission to the contrary, the customer should drive all of the work that your organization performs. Even where a reasonable strategic plan is in place and well-communicated, this "customer-oriented" requirements analysis can be appropriate in determining the cost-effectiveness of an activity.

This requires a definition of who the "customer" is.

For the purposes of requirements analysis, the "customer" is defined as the person or group who gives the organization money to perform its services.

Generally speaking, at for-profit institutions, there are two groups of people who fall into this definition of "customers": (1) people who buy the customer's product, and (2) the company's stockholders.

Under this definition, the customer for the Information Services Department is *not* the employee in Accounting who needs a system developed or modified. The question for requirements analysis purposes is, does the paying customer benefit from changing or developing that system.

Similarly, the customer for a government lobbying organization is the person who pays them to do the lobbying. It is not the group of legislators or administrators being lobbied.

This definition is only for the purpose of requirements analysis, and only where the strategic plan does not provide a full and complete basis for assessing the validity of requirements. The purpose of this definition is not to discourage information systems workers from considering their fellow employees in other departments as customers in providing them with support. In fact, for quality control purposes, employees should think exactly along those lines.

For the purposes of requirements analysis, however, the definition of customer must be narrowed. If the definition of customer is broadened to include all those for whom the company performs a service, then requirements analysis fails. All activity performed by any organization can be justified on the basis that it is performed for someone's benefit somewhere. As a consequence, requirements analysis should include only paying customers.

However, requirements analysis considers both direct service to the customer and indirect service as valid. An activity that directly benefits the customer is a valid requirement, and so is indirect service to the customer.

For example, a stenographer who is preparing a report for his or her boss is indirectly serving the customer if the boss intends to ultimately provide that report to a customer, or if that report helps the boss serve the customer more responsively. If the report is a term paper for the boss's night school class, the requirement is invalid (because the boss is not a customer under our definition), and the activity should be eliminated.

Similarly, budgeting and personnel departments generally perform services that are for the benefit of internal employees: preparing budgets and assisting in internal human resource matters. Without services such as these, it would be impossible for the rest of the company to serve the customer efficiently. Therefore, the customer may be an indirect beneficiary of the activity—but indirect benefit can still be a valid requirement.

All of the requirements underlying an activity should be checked against the requirements and desires of your organization's customers and potential customers. It is obviously in your customers' interest that you maintain a smooth-running and cost-efficient organization in order to provide your product with maximum responsiveness.

> If an activity doesn't make money for the company, then the customer doesn't need it.

Just because an activity is being done for a customer doesn't necessarily mean that there is a valid underlying requirement for the work. Sometimes an organization can go too far in its responsiveness to customers. Serving the customer at all costs can cripple an organization as quickly as ignoring the customer. An examination of the profitability of an activity is appropriate under requirements analysis.

In order to do a good job, company employees usually convince themselves that the activity they perform is highly desired by the customer or is otherwise important to the company. Unfortunately, they often have no objective proof for that belief, and, in fact, that belief may not be true. The best proof that can be provided of the need for an activity is a clear showing that the activity is profitable for the company.

Profitability can be measured in several ways:

- *Direct profitability,* where it can be proven that the income associated with an activity is greater than the cost. An example of this analysis would be an informal financial statement showing that the income associated with the sale of horse-drawn buggies was $10 million, and the cost of those buggies was $6 million, resulting in a profit to the company of $4 million.

- *Indirect profitability,* where it can be shown that— although the cost associated with the activity is greater than the income—there are other indirect profits that justify that activity. Therefore, a company may manufacture buggy whips at a loss of $500,000 per year, but can show that without those buggy whips customers would cease buying their highly profitable horse-drawn carriages. In that case, indirect profitability can justify the activity.

- *Intangible profitability,* where the company believes that an intangible value such as "goodwill" adds to the profitability of the company. An example of this type of activity might be the production of public service announcements for the community or sponsorship of charitable events, where the company feels that the activity will make customers feel good about the company and thus make them more likely to buy its products. The decision regarding whether or not sufficient "goodwill" is generated from an activity is highly subjective, and should be made at the highest levels of the organization.

Measuring profitability is an important step in determining whether an activity is truly being conducted for the benefit of the customers and in determining whether that activity is cost-effective.

Inanimate objects and dead presidents shouldn't be driving your organization's activities.

Although it may seem fairly obvious that only a living human being—preferably a customer—can be a valid requirement for a company's activities, it isn't always as obvious as it may seem.

We've already seen how a dead president was running one company. Let's see how a piece of paper was in charge of another.

At a large southwestern utility, the engineering department continually made tedious and time-consuming hand-drawn changes to a large wall map of its system—even though the utility had a highly sophisticated computerized mapping system in place, and that no one had actually used the wall map for anything in years. When we pressed the manager of that department to tell us why they performed this labor-intensive activity, he made several false starts, then paused. "Well," he finally offered, "the map needs it."

A map should not be driving the work that your organization performs. Unless it's a customer.

It is important to check requirement claims for accuracy. Most people take pride in what they do and are eager to find reasons to justify their day-to-day activities. If employees claim that "the president" has demanded that they perform their activity, ask the president. If they state that "company policy" requires that they do what they do, ask to see the policy statement. If they claim that "regulations" require that they perform some function, ask to see a copy of the regulations.

> Don't believe in myths: The "state law syndrome" runs rampant in corporate America.

As with all institutions, myths can develop and carry over into day-to-day operations. One major area for such myth making is state and federal law.

Naturally, it is important for an organization to obey all of the applicable laws and regulations. However, the content of state law is subject to debate, interpretation, and myth. As a consequence, some employees will argue that their activity, which cannot be shown as profitable or necessary to the customer in itself, is required by state law, regulations or federal statute. In many cases, this may not be true, particularly because laws and regulations upon which activities and departments have been built can change or be reinterpreted over time.

The best response to this argument is to review the relevant law or regulation. If necessary, an independent interpretation of the law or regulation may be required.

It may not be enough to rely on the interpretation of the company's legal department to determine the requirements of laws and regulations. At one regulated company, the general counsel required that senior management and the board of directors meet as a group to review and approve every single expenditure made by the company over $50, resulting in a time-consuming and largely useless waste of expensive executive time. Even the general counsel admitted that the exercise was useless from a business perspective, but insisted that "state law" required such a review.

An examination of the state statute revealed that the wording of the law was vague, and a telephone survey revealed that no other company in the state operating under that statute was circulating and reviewing the expenditure data to that detailed an extent. Accordingly, we recommended substantially raising the dollar limit for expenditures requiring senior management and board approval, thus freeing up valuable time for more cost-effective activities. (Alas, our client did not accept this recommendation, and to this day may be conducting long meetings to obtain senior management approval for purchases of staplers and message pads.)

With these rules in place, return to the example of the hypothetical monthly report being circulated to all employees. By interviewing and possibly surveying employees, five different reasons (or requirements) were identified for the publication and distribution of this report.

"The report contains information necessary for the day-to-day operation of the business, such as budget information, sales data, or responses to customer satisfaction surveys."

Is the information necessary for the day-to-day operation of the business? Certainly some circulation of budget information, sales data, and customer survey results is important to continue the effective running of the business and customer responsiveness. But how much is too much? Many companies spend unnecessary dollars on large reports that are widely circulated, when managers simply turn to the last page to look at the bottom line. If managers only need a few data points from the report, there is little sense in circulating the entire report. Reprogram the computer to circulate a summary report, saving paper as well as circulation and management review time.

If the information is necessary, must the report be circulated to all employees? A significant amount of time and expense can be reduced if the amount of paper circulated to all employees is eliminated.

These questions can be addressed by further examining the requirement: Why is the information necessary? How is it used? How does the customer benefit from every employee having this information? Wouldn't the customer benefit more from reducing the cost of putting out this report, thus reducing the cost of your product?

"The employee who prepares and distributes the report is a personal friend of a member of your board of directors, and the president feels that he has to be given some kind of a job to do."

This requirement may be a corporate myth, particularly if it hasn't been confirmed by the president. Some employees are skillful at convincing their colleagues that they are well-connected and therefore entitled to remain on the payroll even though they don't perform valuable work for the company. Often this simply isn't true and can be checked simply by asking the president about it. In the context of a comprehensive review of the organization for the purpose of reducing costs, senior executives are seldom upset by such questions—particularly if it gives them an opportunity to put this type of myth to rest.

On some occasions, however, senior managers have openly admitted that personnel were put on the payroll for political reasons such as these. Naturally, the underlying requirement for the work is completely invalid: Although the board member is a "customer" for the purpose of our definition, the service being provided to its customers does not include guaranteed peer employment. How is a sensitive situation such as this handled?

Remember: This is a rigorous review of the *activities* performed by the organization. If the activities being performed by an employee are appropriate to the organization, and the requirements for that work are all the result of customer desires or strategic goals, then the fact that the person who performs them is a friend of a board member is irrelevant.

On the other hand, if the functions performed by an employee do not have a valid underlying requirement, the function should be eliminated, irrespective of whether or not the person performing that function is politically well-connected. Final decisions on all recommendations, of course, are ultimately made or approved by senior management.

"The report facilitates communication among employees and departments, thereby encouraging team building and consensus within your organization."

Team building, communication, and consensus are fashionable business terms these days. It is arguable, however, whether much of this activity is driven by customer needs or strategic goals and objectives.

Most times, when fashionable phrases or "buzz words" are used to justify an activity, the activity is probably of limited usefulness to the corporation. Look for phrases such as "contributes to total quality" or "creates consensus," and be aware of more recent business trends. Business in the United States is particularly sensitive to fads and fashions, and can go too far in accommodating the latest style.

It is possible to be overly cynical on this point, however. Where consensus and team building clearly contributes to the overall operation and effectiveness of the organization, an activity that encourages consensus and communication may be valuable. Judge the activity against the basic goals and objectives of the company, and when in doubt, seek guidance from senior management regarding the value of the activity.

"The report has been prepared and distributed for the past twenty years, and no one has ever complained about it or argued that it was unnecessary."

Sounds funny? Believe it or not, this is a surprisingly common reason that activities and functions are performed by many organizations, particularly organizations that have been in existence over a long period of time. We human beings tend not to rethink our established patterns. Corporate activities have their own kind of inertia. Once established, they can be hard to change or eliminate.

Naturally, this requirement in itself is not valid. In the absence of any other more valid requirement, the activity should be eliminated.

"By state law, the report must be approved and signed by the president of the company, who wants to make sure that all company employees have an opportunity to review and comment."

Does state law really require that this report be approved and signed? What does state law actually say? What do companies operating under similar state laws do? Can a summary report be submitted? Is it really necessary that all of the employees review the report? Can it be circulated to only senior managers? Perhaps even select senior managers? Answers to questions such as these can determine whether the report is necessary.

Even assuming that our hypothetical monthly report passes the requirements test and is a valid activity for the organization, other questions emerge. Can the report be prepared in a more cost-effective manner? Can the report be printed on both sides of the page, thus reducing paper costs? Can it be stapled rather than bound, thereby reducing printing costs? Better yet, can it be transmitted directly to the computer terminals of employees, thus eliminating production and printing costs entirely? Can the cost of distribution be reduced? Questions such as these are answered through "reengineering": An examination of how the company performs the work that it does, and how improvements can be made.

4

How Do We Do What We Do? (Reengineering)

> Doing the same work twice doesn't necessarily get it done any better.

Early in the 1980s, one large company prided itself on not having a public relations department. "The quality of our work and the dedication of our employees is so strong and so obvious, it speaks for itself," their president told us. "We have no requirement for a public relations function. There's no need for us to devote a lot of effort defending ourselves to the press."

Imagine our surprise (and his) when our review of activities indicated that nearly seven percent of the total work effort at that organization was devoted to . . . public relations!

As it turned out, many of the executives and managers at the organization disagreed with the president's philosophy, and disregarded the company's strategic direction by creating individual public relations departments throughout the organization. The district field offices each had their own public relations functions, as did the customer service and marketing departments. As a result, severe duplication occurred in public relations. Several employees were independently responsible for coordination of media inquiries, and in some minor cases contradictory information was given to the press by two spokespersons acting unilaterally.

While the company's general thrust was correct—the president was good at interacting with the press, wrote his own speeches, and due to the noncontroversial nature of the company's business they were at little risk of a major public relations emergency—the company ultimately decided that a coordinating position should be developed to serve as the focal point for public relations efforts. This coordination resulted in a reduced overall effort for public relations functions and improved control over material being sent to customers, legislators, and the media.

If your company is overstaffed, chances are it is because people are making work for themselves. "Make work" in a business context falls into several categories:

- *Filling a vacuum.* Like the employees in the company without a public relations department, managers and executives may disagree with the company's strategic direction. Accordingly, they may create "satellite" functions within their own departments, which can often duplicate the satellite functions other managers create. The classic example of this type of activity is in information systems: A manager, unhappy with the service that the centralized Information Services Department provides, trains his or her own employees in computer science and turns them loose to develop software independent of the corporate computer group. If enough dissatisfied managers create their own isolated computer departments, the company can wind up with several employees independently developing similar but incompatible computer programs.

- *Redoing work.* At the engineering department of a large midwestern utility, some work was designed two or three times by independent engineers, then reviewed by still others to combine the best elements into an optimal design. The stated reason for this duplication was to ensure quality. The real reason was that the engineering department had far too many engineers, and they couldn't all be kept busy through the traditional system of one engineer, one project.

- *Overapproval.* Compensation systems at many companies encourage the artificial promotion of employees in order to increase their salaries. Therefore, an employee who is underpaid often gets promoted to a managerial level, even though there are few people to supervise. Those few employees sometimes wind up oversupervised by their new manager, who reviews their work in excruciating detail and sends it back for trivial changes. Such overapproval wastes corporate time and money—not to mention the effect that it can have on the morale of the oversupervised employees.

- *Computerphobia.* This is a rapidly disappearing phenomenon but one that continues to exist. The manager who has grown up without computers fears the new technologies, insisting instead on doing everything with spreadsheet and pencil. Five employees do the work that one data processor could perform in a properly computerized organization.

- *Gold plating.* Your employees genuinely want to do the best possible job that they can for their customers. Sometimes they can go overboard. One print shop insisted on putting formal binders and covers on all reports over fifty pages, even those that were only intended for internal distribution. The company was able to save a surprising amount of money by mandating that documents were only to be stapled, unless prior approval for formal binding was obtained from the department manager.

"Reengineering" is the term currently given to the painstaking and time-consuming task of reviewing and revising the way things are done in your organization.

Often, it involves flowcharting the process, identifying redundancy and unnecessary activities in the flow chart, and streamlining the process. But there are a few hints and short cuts that can streamline the process, and still result in cost savings for your organization.

> Work should be performed by the organization in order to keep customers satisfied; work should not be created by the organization in order to keep employees satisfied.

One large insurance company was divided into several smaller units. These units competed with each other in the market, providing different types of health insurance to potential customers.

Each unit had a separate department responsible for provider contracting, which involved negotiating specially discounted rates with local doctors and hospitals in the insurance company's service territory. And each unit insisted on having its own provider contractors who separately negotiated with each hospital for the best deal. Consequently, each doctor, clinic, and hospital in the area would be visited by up to three different representatives of the same company, all interested in getting the best bargain. And, as it turned out, the doctors and hospitals would often wind up providing three different rates, one to each unit of the same company!

The company was losing out, of course, by not combining its three units and negotiating a bulk volume discount that most likely would have been even greater than the best discount negotiated by any one of the individual units. But from a reengineering standpoint, unnecessary activity resulted because several company employees were negotiating with the same hospitals for the same thing. Because the provider contracting function required a considerable amount of "windshield time"—time driving from one hospital or clinic to another—the company sent many employees to spend time driving back and forth across the freeways and toll roads in their territory.

Companies often create unnecessary work for themselves. Some managers are sticklers for detail and want to check each work product several different times, using several different employees. Still others, who are managers of field offices or line organizations, don't trust the corporate offices and want to develop their own systems and procedures rather than rely on the corporate systems already in place. And, perhaps most common, is the manager who creates work because he or she does not want to fire a moderately competent employee who no longer performs a valuable service for the organization.

The best way to examine the work process to determine unnecessary work is to create a flow chart. Trace a given activity from the moment the request for work is generated until the moment the work is completed. Examining that flow chart can provide a guide to unnecessary approvals, duplication in product development, or unnecessary steps or stages in the work process.

In its simplest form, a flow chart is a diagram that summarizes work flows and the outcome of decision processes:

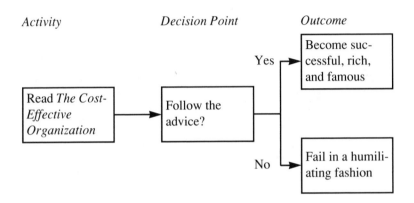

One way to construct a flow chart is to plot time on the horizontal axis, and departments/individuals on the vertical axis:

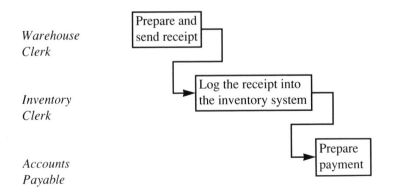

Once the flow chart is constructed in this manner, it can be examined to determine whether there are opportunities for improvement:

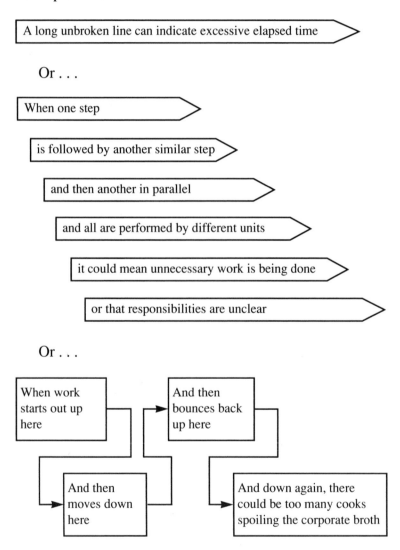

A long unbroken line can indicate excessive elapsed time

Or . . .

When one step

is followed by another similar step

and then another in parallel

and all are performed by different units

it could mean unnecessary work is being done

or that responsibilities are unclear

Or . . .

When work starts out up here

And then bounces back up here

And then moves down here

And down again, there could be too many cooks spoiling the corporate broth

Processes can be unnecessarily complex for many reasons. For example, one reason that so many approvals are required may be that some employees are anxious to justify the importance of their positions.

> Managers in many organizations continually engage in a desperate struggle to use important verbs such as "manage," "delegate," "approve," and "supervise" in the written description of a relatively low-level position in order to increase the salary level authorized for that position.

It is very difficult to develop clear and consistent organization-wide guidelines for compensation. Some such guidelines often base compensation in large part on the duties of the job, as stated in the job's formal position description. The result: Position descriptions throughout the organization hum with pretentious buzz words, as mid-level managers and entry-level employees struggle to make their jobs sound more important than they really are.

Attempts to manipulate job descriptions do little more than damage the accuracy of those descriptions, which have relatively few cost implications. Another element used in determining a "fair" compensation level, however, has had a more serious impact on cost. Compensation also is often based on the amount of budget managed and number of employees supervised. The more money you spend, and the more employees you supervise, the larger your pay.

When managers caught on to the rules of this game, it resulted in the rise of the "mini-managers"—employees whose organizations were juggled slightly to give them one or two nominal employees to supervise in order to increase their base rate of compensation. Often, no real supervision was required; the appearance of an organization reporting to the employee was created to justify a higher salary for that employee.

No wonder, then, that managers in companies throughout the world engage in bitter political battles to outspend their colleagues and overbuild their own empires in order to increase their prestige within the organization—and improve their quality of life outside it.

There are two clues that indicate that your company may be a victim of this phenomenon:

- *Narrow spans of control throughout the organization.*
  In examining the organization chart, you may find
  that there are numerous "pockets" of one person
  reporting to one person reporting to one person, or
  two reporting to one reporting to one. These narrow
  spans of control indicate that the compensation system may be resulting in unnecessary managerial
  positions.

- *End-of-the-fiscal-year spending sprees.* Where managers are rewarded for the large size of their budgets, they will tend to spend all of their leftover funds before the close of the fiscal year, rather than return those funds and run the risk of a lower budget in the next year. A pattern of spending that peaks at year-end is a preliminary indication that at least some of that spending is unnecessary.

Look for these symptoms, and chances are good that the disease is a compensation system that rewards empire building. First, eliminate the unnecessary spending and managerial activity; and second, change the compensation system.

When this happens, changes will result in the process or the way activities are performed. When unnecessary and redundant layers are built into the organization, almost invariably they lead to unnecessary and redundant activities. Documents that once were quickly approved by a single manager, for example, now require several approvals, one in each link of the chain. Decisions that were quickly made now take several days or weeks as they work their way up the corporate ladder, often killing or dismembering bright and original ideas that were generated deep within the lower rungs of the organization. By eliminating the redundancy, you can eliminate activities and improve the ability of the organization to respond quickly to new ideas.

Compensation systems aren't the only reason for unnecessary work, of course. Sometimes the cause of inefficient processes is a common ailment: Fear of the unknown.

> *Byte Fright:* The overwhelming fear that, the first time you sit down to use the company's computer, you will wipe out the entire corporate data base and destroy every computer system your company uses.

Our recent visit to the finance department of a medium-sized company was like a trip backwards in time. Accountants hunched wearily over their spreadsheets, writing numbers into the columns and adding the totals. When the totals didn't balance, the accountants sighed, erasers scratched against paper, and the process started anew.

In one corner, a woman with a look of long-embedded frustration carefully scrutinized two piles of papers, attempting to match each invoice in one pile with its corresponding purchase order in the other pile. When she was able to find two that matched, she then went over to a third pile of papers to see if she could find the warehouse receipt to match the invoice and purchase order. When—eureka!—she was finally able to match an invoice with a purchase order with a warehouse receipt, she trudged over to a typewriter and typed out a check to the supplier.

But the ultimate in frustration was reserved for the payroll clerk. Three hundred employees in the company had requested that their payroll checks be deposited directly into their checking accounts. At most computerized companies, direct deposit involves a simple set of keystrokes that signals the bank's computer to credit the employee's account with the net amount of the paycheck.

At this company, however, "direct deposit" meant that the payroll clerk would write all the checks, fill out the deposit slips, take them to the bank downstairs—and then wait in line at the teller's window!

Shades of the 1950s! The only things missing, it seemed, were quill pens and green eyeshades.

The manager of this accounting department admitted that he wasn't comfortable with computers and didn't have one in his office. "I've never really learned to use them," he said. "But I encourage my employees to find uses for the computer," he added, pointing to a solitary and nearly obsolete personal computer out in the main hallway. The computer was rusty from neglect, and further discussions with other employees in the accounting department made clear what was already obvious: Those employees, recognizing their manager's intense dislike of computers, did not want to risk his wrath by using them.

Even in this day and age of the proliferating personal computer, there are companies that are insufficiently computerized to meet the challenges presented by their more technological competitors.

Some tools and techniques to determine whether a function or activity in your organization is insufficiently computerized include the following:

- A simple "visual overview" can assist in determining whether a process is excessively manual. (In other words, look around.) If there appears to be a large number of handwritten spreadsheets and vertical files in areas where computerization is expected, such as accounting and procurement, that may be a preliminary signal that a computer system could improve processes and save money. This is particularly true where there are few computer terminals or personal computers apparent within that department.

- A review of the process through interviews with relevant personnel can show if activities are taking too long. In most cases, department personnel are well aware of the computer options for their functions and are eager to share those options in the hope of someday obtaining and implementing them.

- "Best practices analysis," a fancy term given to the age-old process of talking to businesses similar to yours, to determine how they perform their functions and whether their way is better than yours. When examining computerization, the issue is whether other similar businesses have successfully and profitably computerized functions that you are still performing manually.

- At large organizations, "best practices analysis" can be done internally. For example, where you have several customer service departments or field offices, each may have its own way of recording customer contacts or measuring performance. If one department, unit, or office has developed its own highly successful personal computer-based system for performing an activity, that system might also be valuable to similar units or departments organization-wide. Thus, you are identifying the best practice in your organization and implementing that practice throughout the company.

Best practices analysis can be used to analyze all processes, not just information systems development, and is therefore an important tool in process analysis. Although some companies have used trickery in the past to obtain information on their competition, that type of skullduggery is not necessary for a successful benchmarking effort. Best practices can be determined from examining businesses in unrelated fields, or by looking at companies in related fields but, for geographical or other reasons, are not in direct competition. One electric utility did a comprehensive best practices analysis by examining unrelated businesses such as an overnight courier and an airline, as well as other utilities in distant parts of the United States.

In this time of ever-emerging computer technology, there is little excuse for manual spreadsheet development or matching of documents. In fact, the most cost-effective organizations are rapidly evolving toward the "paperless bureaucracy," communicating almost entirely by terminal—often communicating from one machine to another and eliminating human interaction where unnecessary.

No matter what the attitude toward computers, however, virtually all employees want to do a good job of satisfying the needs of their employers and customers. And that may create as much unnecessary work as anything else.

> Yes, providing high quality service to your customers is important. But keeping your price down is the ultimate customer service.

We came up with what we thought was an easy cost-reduction idea for one customer service department. For years, that department overstaffed its customer service telephone lines on the theory that "our customers should be able to talk to someone immediately without having to wait." A nice philosophy, at least in theory. But the result was that up to a dozen telephone representatives sat idle most of the day, waiting to answer calls during those relatively brief periods when the number of calls peaked.

Our recommendation was relatively simple. The customer service department should (a) train their telephone representatives in other tasks such as responding to correspondence and processing small invoices, in order to give them work to perform during off-peak times, and (b) implement a philosophy that could require customers to wait on hold for up to thirty seconds for a telephone representative during particularly busy periods.

Survey data from similar companies showed that a thirty second delay had little impact on overall customer satisfaction, and our recommendation also entailed a consumer education program that instructed customers on the best times to call for service. Moreover, our recommendation would result in a net savings to the company of $250,000 a year. Still, the recommendation ran into intense roadblocks—not from customers, but from employees.

Not only did the employees involved with customer service object to the idea of making customers wait, they even objected to the concept of training telephone representatives for other work. "You're sacrificing the quality of our telephone service," one customer service manager argued, "when our reps have to concentrate on other projects, even for part of the day."

The vice president of customer service was particularly adamant, threatening to quit if our recommendations were implemented and customer service deteriorated as a result.

(After our recommendation was implemented, the vice president failed to follow through on this threat.)

No, there was no featherbedding or turf-building going on. These employees were so committed to the concept of providing customer service that they had forgotten a key point: providing your product at the lowest possible cost is one of your most important customer services.

When an employee's career has been devoted to providing high-quality accounting services, legal services, or engineering services to the company, the employee can often lose sight that those services represent a cost to the organization. Most employees want to do absolutely the best possible job they can for the company that hired them.

The need to satisfy customer demand at any cost can reach extreme proportions. At another company, a vice president objected strongly to our recommendation to eliminate certain product demonstrations that appeared to contribute little to the company's marketing effort. "Those are educational presentations, and our customers want them," she argued. Would she object if we recommended simply cutting back on the number of such demonstrations? Yes. Well, would she mind if we recommended cutting back on the apparently large number of handouts provided during those demonstrations? Yes. What about eliminating the snacks and drinks that were provided at those demonstrations? She was appalled!

But what did the customers, who were ultimately paying the bill for these demonstrations, think? Our focus group interviews with customers indicated that most of them knew little or nothing of these demonstrations, did not consider them to be of value, and would prefer to see the price of the product provided by that company lowered.

Customer service is important. But it is also important to look for examples of "gold plating"—where the value of the service provided to the customer is exceeded by the cost of providing that service—and identify opportunities to perform that service at a lower cost.

If you've taken your organization through functional analysis, requirements analysis, and reengineering, then at this point you have developed a series of recommendations that will streamline your organization and make it run more efficiently and cost-effectively. The next step is to determine whether or not there is an opportunity to perform activities less expensively by reducing their inherent costs.

5

How Much Do We Pay
for What We Do?
(Cost Analysis)

> If your competition has lower prices than you, maybe it's because they pay less for their services than you do.

We once did a quick analysis for one company regarding their custodial service. On one side of the page, we calculated the cost of performing janitorial and custodial services in-house, and on the other side we calculated the cost of using a local cleaning service for that work. Our review of those figures indicated that the company was well-served by continuing to perform its custodial work in-house, so we crumpled up the worksheet and threw it in the wastebasket.

Unfortunately, an alert custodian saw the analysis fall out of the wastebasket while emptying it. The custodian fished it out, and brought it to the custodian's union hall! It took several rounds of meetings to convince the union that firing all the janitors was a trial balloon that had long since popped.

Most work that is performed in-house could, theoretically, be done by contractors. And most work performed outside could be brought in-house. An apparent trend in recent years has been to contract out work that has traditionally been done internally, thus reducing the cost of work performed for the organization—both in terms of salary and administrative burden.

It is also possible that the company may be overpaying for work performed in-house, particularly where compensation is largely a function of seniority. The issue of compensation is especially complex, and an employee charged with reviewing functions throughout an organization probably cannot do a careful analysis of all compensation levels. But there are a couple of examinations that can be performed to determine whether the company is overpaying for the services it receives.

Some work (such as janitorial service) may be more cost-effective if done by an outside contractor. Other types of work (such as legal services) may be less expensive if done in-house.

There is an analysis—somewhat oversimplified—for determining, on an initial basis, whether work should be performed in-house or by outside contractors. This is the analysis (best performed on the back of an envelope), which assumes no one-time capital costs or expenses, and relatively steady costs from year to year:

EXPENSE FOR PERFORMING THE WORK IN-HOUSE:

Annual wage cost:	$ _____
Annual benefits cost:	$ _____
Annual incremental overhead costs:	$ _____
Other incremental annual costs:	$ _____
TOTAL IN-HOUSE COST:	$ _____

EXPENSE FOR CONTRACTING THE WORK OUT:

Number of hours needed to perform the job:	_____
Multiplied by the hourly rate for the job:	$ _____
Equals the annual contracting cost:	$ _____
Other annualized contracting costs:	$ _____
TOTAL CONTRACTING COST:	$ _____

RISKS TO BE CONSIDERED (IF ANY):

MECHANISMS TO CONTAIN THOSE RISKS:

Where the cost of performing work in-house exceeds the cost of contracting it out, the work should generally be performed outside. When the cost of contracting exceeds the cost of doing it yourself, the work should be done inside the company. Where there are uneven expenses from year to year or one-time costs associated with one option or the other, more sophisticated financial analysis such as discounted cash flow or internal rate of return can be applied.

At one company, it made sense to bring certain legal work in-house, even though there were certain built-in inefficiencies to that option. The analysis was as follows:

Annual total cost to perform the work in-house:	$75,000
Annual total cost to hire outside contractors:	
Number of hours required: 1000	
Hourly rate: $250	
Total Annual Cost (1000×250):	$250,000
Amount saved by doing the work in-house:	$175,000

In this example, the company brought in a full-time lawyer to perform legal work for the company that could have been done by an outside law firm in about one-half of a year (1000 hours). The full-time lawyer would work about 2000 hours per year. Yet, because the hourly rate for the in-house lawyer was substantially lower than that of the outside law firm, the company saved money by allowing the internal lawyer to spent more time doing that work. (Incidentally, your independent law firm should be referred to as "outside counsel." Although it is perfectly acceptable to refer to your internal legal staff as "in-house lawyers," your law firm may object to being referred to as "outhouse lawyers.")

There are often risks associated with bringing work in-house or contracting it out. One company was very concerned about contracting out its janitorial and custodial services, even though such contracting would save nearly $100,000 a year. Other companies in the area, it seemed, had a problem with the quality of service provided by local cleaning and building maintenance companies. The company controlled that risk by establishing certain quality control mechanisms, such as routine inspections and informal satisfaction surveys of employees, and providing the results of those reviews to the supplying company. The few problems that the company had with the cleaning service soon disappeared. Even the janitors themselves had few problems with the switch, because most of them simply went to work for the contracting firm.

In many cases, when contracting out work, the companies have taken steps to ensure that the contracting firm would retain the employees that would be let go by the company. This seems, in most cases, to make good business sense as well as being good for the morale of the company.

Be careful when stepping into the minefield of compensation.

It is difficult to conduct a comprehensive review of compensation levels to determine whether they are reasonable, because it is a complex and emotional issue—particularly for those who are receiving the compensation.

Rarely does a cost-reduction review result in wholesale reductions in salaries or other compensation, reductions that result from a comprehensive review of the job market. Generally speaking, wholesale salary reductions occur in the cost-reduction effort only when there is an arbitrary edict from senior management to reduce salaries by some predetermined amount. ("We're reducing all salaries by ten percent, effective immediately.") Such across-the-board reductions, in salaries as well as staffing, are a bad long-term idea. If your salaries aren't market-based, your best people will leave for other jobs. And there may be bitterness among your remaining employees, who see their peers from other companies and former colleagues who have jumped ship make more money, while they stay frozen at their arbitrarily-determined level.

On the other hand, overpaying employees isn't always appreciated either. These "golden handcuffs" can chain your employees to organizations or jobs where they aren't happy but are doomed to remain because of the ever-improving lifestyles and expectations of themselves and their families.

There are two examinations you can perform to ensure that compensation appears reasonable.

- Review the system used to set compensation levels to ensure that they include surveys of compensation at other companies. Review that survey data to determine where your company stands relative to others. If your company is consistently on the high side of the compensation scale, and there is no stated company policy calling for higher-than-average compensation as a mechanism for attracting a higher-than-average caliber of employee, there may be an opportunity to adjust salaries.

- Review compensation across your organization. Are secretaries on the same pay scale everywhere? If you work for a holding company that has several operating companies, are the pay scales the same at each operating company? If not, is there a reason for the discrepancy?

The same type of analysis holds true for the benefits package as well. By comparing the benefits your company offers to those provided by other companies, and by exploring the new techniques that companies are implementing to reduce ever-increasing benefits costs (particularly those related to health insurance), your company can end up with a considerable cost savings.

To the extent that your review does identify opportunities for cost reduction through changes in the compensation schedule, consider phasing in those changes. This would involve "freezing" compensation at current levels, allowing inflation to gradually bring overpaid salary scales into line. But never underestimate the emotionalism inherent in the salary decisions your company makes.

> Identify the biggest item in your budget, and examine it carefully.

In many cost-reduction efforts, the company rigorously reviews all the activities in the company, then comes up with recommendations that save a few thousand dollars here and a few thousand there. That's fine. Many highly successful cost-reduction programs have been made up of literally hundreds of such recommendations.

But don't neglect the big ticket items.

In many businesses, the bulk of the spending is dedicated to just a few items. For example, in the business of generating and transmitting electricity, the biggest annual expense tends to be the cost of fuel. In the insurance industry, claims, by far, account for the largest expense. At health care clinics, it's the cost of outside providers such as doctors and hospitals. At retail outlets, ranging from department stores to auto dealers, it's the cost of inventory.

It's often easier to save money by making a few minor adjustments to these big ticket items than to make radical changes to several of the smaller activities that your organization performs.

One electric utility, for example, kept a forty-five to sixty-day supply of coal on site at its power plant. However, historical records of coal use at that plant and a review of industry practices showed that a thirty-day supply would have been more than ample. By reducing the on-site supply to thirty days, the company enjoyed the benefit of a one-time reduction in expenses as well as the income associated with investing that new revenue for a healthy rate of return.

In an effective cost-reduction program, at least one employee should be assigned the responsibility for becoming intimately familiar with the big-ticket items in the budget, working with employees throughout the company to fully understand that expense and developing ways to reduce it.

The cycle is almost complete. We've examined what the organization does, how it does what it does, why it does it, and how much it costs to get it done. As a result of this analysis, you've no doubt discovered a number of ways to streamline processes, improve productivity efficiency, get along with a different number of employees, and maybe even a different type of organization. Organizational analysis is one additional part, and only a part, of your comprehensive review of costs.

6
Why Have We Organized Things This Way? (Organizational Analysis)

> Trying to save on business expenses simply by redrawing the organization chart is like trying to save on household expenses simply by rearranging the furniture.

Too many organizations feel that they can save money by eliminating managers and combining departments, thereby creating fewer boxes on the organization chart. But redrawing the organization chart is always the last step in a successful cost-reduction program.

One large organization calculated, on the back of one of its envelopes, that it could save $10 million a year simply by removing one level in its bloated organization. Happily, it went to work redrawing the organization and setting up procedures for eliminating that level. Chaos quickly resulted.

Contrary to popular myth, you cannot save one penny for your company by redrawing the boxes on your organization chart. "Reorganization" and "restructuring" are not necessarily the same as "cost reduction."

Sure, you can cross out some of the boxes on your organization chart or arbitrarily increase the "spans of control" so that managers are responsible for managing more employees with a resulting need for fewer managers. Or you can eliminate all the "assistant-to" or staff positions.

But in the absence of a reduction in the amount of work being done by the company (in other words, without first figuring out what is being done, for whom, how, and can it be done more cheaply), reducing the number of boxes on the organization chart simply results in the same amount of work being done by fewer people. This, in turn, results in poorly performed work, lower productivity, decreased morale, and an ever-increasing backlog of work that is likely to be ultimately translated into staffing and cost increases.

In the case of our large and well-known company, their exercise in cost reduction through "boxology" (rearranging boxes on the organization chart) ultimately led to cost increases and then to a commitment to restructure the organization by first looking at functions and costs.

Although redrawing the organization chart in itself does not result in any cost savings, organizational analysis can be used as an effective support tool in requirements and process analysis. It answers no questions, but can point the way toward opportunities for possible cost reduction and efficiency improvements.

> Where there are too many managers, there is probably too much unnecessary work being performed.

Managers tend to create work for their subordinates. After all, managers are partly judged on their ability to keep their subordinates busy. If employees are seen slacking off, their managers are quickly accused of improper supervision.

But a cost-effective organization should not create unnecessary work for itself. All employees must perform work that carries out the goals and objectives of the organization, and overmanagement creates a barrier to achieving that kind of efficiency.

The organization chart cannot, by itself, show whether or not unnecessary work is being performed. It cannot even show whether a given position or function is being overmanaged. Often, people who are shown as "managers" on the organization chart do little managing.

But the organization chart can be a valuable resource for determining—on a preliminary basis—if too many managers exist. To examine what an organization chart can show, consider the following example:

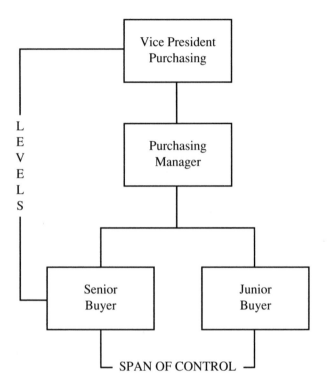

The "span of control" is the number of direct reports that a position has. In this case, the Vice President of Purchasing has a span of control of one, because only one position—the Purchasing Manager—reports directly to the vice president. The Purchasing Manager has a span of control of two, because two positions report directly to the Purchasing Manager.

The "levels" are the number of layers in the organization. There are three levels in this organization: One at the Vice President's level, one at the Manager's level, and one at the Buyer level.

This hypothetical department has only four employees, yet has three organizational levels and a span of control of two. The Vice President of Marketing has a span of control of only one, assuming that the Marketing Manager is the only direct report to the vice president. In short, there are probably too many queen bees and not enough workers, with the following probable outcomes:

- The vice president is probably overpaid because executives who are compensated at the vice president level typically have responsibility for far more than three employees.

- The vice president and manager probably perform similar work, with some amount of redundancy.

- The vice president and/or manager may create unnecessary work for themselves and their subordinates to perform and manage, in order to justify their continued employment at relatively high levels of the company.

- The buyers are probably oversupervised with their requisitions requiring numerous unnecessary rewrites to respond to the comments generated by their two supervisors.

If all this is true, there are a number of opportunities to reduce the number of activities and the cost associated with the purchasing function in this organization. However, the organization chart in and of itself does not prove that these outcomes are necessarily true. The following may also be true:

- All of the employees on this chart perform meaning-ful and important work for the organization, which cannot be reduced or eliminated without seriously harming the company and its ability to provide effec-tive customer service.

- The organization must have someone with the title of "vice president" in charge of the purchasing function in order to negotiate effectively with certain large customers. Accordingly, the company has bestowed the title of "Vice President of Purchasing" on a rela-tively low-level employee, whose compensation has been adjusted downward to reflect reduced responsi-bility when compared to other vice presidents in the organization.

- The purchasing manager's position is mistitled. That employee does little purchasing work and almost entirely performs special projects for the president of the organization. The placement of that position in this organization is merely a convenience.

- The vice president is also a working buyer, spending little time supervising the other two buyers who know their jobs well.

If these are all true, then—whatever other failings this organization may have—excess staffing is not necessarily among them. Although one can quibble with some of the organizational placement and titling, there is little opportunity for cost reduction through reorganization in this hypothetical department.

> The organization chart can serve as a guide to cost-reduction opportunities—but can't be treated as conclusive evidence of inefficiency.

It is tempting to think that, because an organization has narrow spans of control and a number of redundant layers of management, there is a lot of "fat" in the organization that can be shaved off with resulting cost savings. And, in fact, that is generally the case with such an organization. However, the organization chart in and of itself proves nothing.

Narrow spans of control and excessive organization levels are created for a reason. Those reasons may include:

- Specialized fields that require close supervision. A manager responsible for training in a highly technical or complex field, for example, may be able to supervise only one or two individuals.

- Management development and succession planning. Where there are no readily available successors for a key position, the company may choose to place an individual in a one-on-one organizational relationship, or with managerial responsibility over a limited number of employees, in order to train and develop that person for a planned or possible vacancy.

Of course, in many cases excessive layers and narrow spans of control also mean overmanagement. In these cases, supervisors may subject the work of their subordinates to constant and needless review and rereview, with the final work product then working itself up the chain of command for more review, comment, and rework. Such an organization lends itself to streamlining and increased cost-effectiveness.

In any event, it is impossible to tell simply from looking at the organization chart whether a department or unit is overstaffed. Such a decision requires a careful review of all the activities performed by that organization. Once that review has taken place, however, an organization with narrow spans of control and excessive levels can be streamlined into a new organization, characterized by fewer chains of command and easier communication.

> When changing the number of people in the organi-
> zation, keep the organization's basic goals and
> strategies in mind.

You've looked at the organization chart, determined that spans of control within the organization seem unusually narrow, and then conducted the analysis of activities, processes, and requirements that is entailed in an effective cost-reduction analysis. Those analyses confirmed that there are too many managers in that department, and that you can therefore reduce the number of employees without affecting the activities performed by that department. This is where organizational redesign comes in.

You now have an organization of, say, ten people (as opposed to the fourteen you had before you eliminated unnecessary activities). Creating a new organizational structure for those ten people (or hundred, or thousand) is a multistep process:

- Develop some basic rules of organizational structure. These are general guidelines that are used to develop the new organization. For example, your organization structure should try to group like functions together, keep spans of control at the maximum feasible level, and levels of organization at a minimum. Your organization may have some unique rules; for example, don't mix marketing and pricing functions, because marketing people tend to set the prices too low in order to maximize sales.

- Develop a set of criteria for the particular organization you are redesigning. For example, you may want your organization to "provide a centralized point of focus for customer feedback" or "identify a clear organizational point of accountability for cost reduction and cost control."

- Design three or four different organizations that appear to meet each of those criteria.

- Evaluate each of the organizations and determine which does the best job of meeting most of the criteria you've developed.

Suppose, for example, that you've decided that your new Customer Service and Marketing Department should focus on improving the relationships between the company and its customers. In that case, this organization might be totally appropriate:

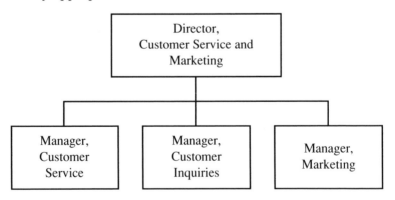

The first two managers are responsible for customer service functions, while only the remaining third manager has responsibility for marketing. There are twice as many managerial resources devoted to customer relations as there are to marketing, reflecting the organization's desire to emphasize strengthening its relationships with existing customers.

If, however, the company's focus is on marketing rather than customer service, the above organization might imply too much focus on customer service at the expense of marketing. The proper organization might then look like this:

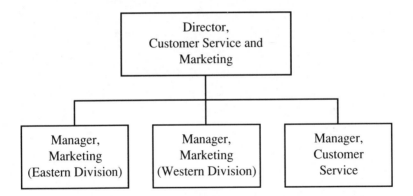

Here there are two managers responsible for marketing and only one with customer service responsibilities. This better reflects the company's emphasis on marketing its products and services.

In neither case does the company save any money by drawing the organization chart one way or the other. The savings came when we decided, earlier on, that the department could do its work with fewer people. The purpose of good organizational design is to "tie a ribbon around the package," so that the newly streamlined organization functions as effectively as possible.

Organization design is an art, not a science.

When you engage in organization design, watch out. By definition, conflict and controversy are sure to follow.

For example, while your Director of Customer Service and Marketing is busily considering how to redesign the Customer Service and Marketing Department, the president of the organization is upstairs thinking about reorganizing the entire company. Customer service and marketing functions may quickly become a smaller cog in the larger considerations faced by the organization's senior management.

There is an almost unlimited number of options that you have in redesigning either your department or your company, and each has its advantages and disadvantages to the customers, stockholders, and employees. By sharing the process, conducting it openly, and by clearly communicating the criteria that the organization is expected to achieve, the optimum organization structure should emerge from long, and often painful, interaction between managers and executives throughout the company.

Now you've got a newly-streamlined organization, with improved processes and greater cost effectiveness—all written down on paper. Now comes the greatest challenge of the whole process: translating those written ideas and thoughts into real-world action.

7

What Happens After Cost Reduction?

> Coming up with good ideas is hard. Implementing them is harder.

What is the result of all this cost-reduction effort? Nothing more than a list of good ideas. Let's look at some of the recommendations from a cost-reduction program that resulted in savings of $50 million a year for the organization that implemented it:

REQUIREMENTS ANALYSIS RESULTS

- Eliminate certain planned capital projects due to the projected downward trend in the demand for their related products

- Consolidate products that conflict/compete with each other in the market

- Eliminate the medical services facility at corporate offices where there are few workplace safety or injury problems and a medical clinic is located nearby

COST ANALYSIS RESULTS

- Increase the number of internal auditors and redirect their focus to improve internal controls

- Eliminate inconsistencies in pay scales to prevent overpaying certain employees

- Offer a "managed care" health insurance option to reduce the cost of employee benefits

- Eliminate high-cost, low-benefit marketing programs

- Drop out of trade associations with high membership dues and low perceived value

- Contract out most functions performed by the corporate secretary, such as mailing out and tabulating proxy statements or managing the dividend reinvestment program

- Contract out the payroll function

- Consolidate three different but similar publications that the company has been preparing for employees: One for all employees, one for managers, and one for retirees

- Use paralegals and law clerks for routine legal duties, reserving lawyers for more complex legal matters and representation at legal proceedings

REENGINEERING RESULTS

- Streamline the performance appraisal process to require fewer reviews and approvals

- Eliminate multiple reception areas in a single location

- Reduce multiple and duplicate records storage activities and locations

- Transfer most data entry functions to the field to eliminate duplication

- Improve the performance and productivity of telephone customer representatives through improved monitoring technology

- Establish minimum/automatic reordering quantities in the warehousing system

- Coordinate planning functions that currently occur independently throughout the organization

- Provide automatic drawing and drafting equipment to engineers to prevent manual drafting and tracing of drawings

ORGANIZATIONAL ANALYSIS RESULTS

- Consolidate training departments in the field to eliminate redundancy

- Eliminate redundant Manager/Deputy Manager/Assistant Manager positions at factories

- Consolidate procurement departments, eliminating redundant activities and allowing the organization to make larger purchases and thereby receive volume discounts

This list—the product of four to five months of intensive effort on the part of over a dozen company employees and a team of consultants—is only the beginning. The next step involves the difficult task of implementing the program and ensuring that the savings associated with the program are achieved on an ongoing basis. And there are several considerations involved with implementation, including the development of an implementation monitoring mechanism and communications plan, design of an employee redeployment program, and an overall redirection of the organization to reflect the greater cost-reduction emphasis.

> When it comes to implementing a cost-reduction plan, trust your employees—but verify the results.

It's not surprising that cost reduction isn't natural for most business managers. The corporate culture for the past several decades has been to spend money, build empires, and thereby grow the business. To cut costs is counterintuitive, and the company must continually reinforce the idea that the company will make the changes necessary to reduce costs. Otherwise, employees will adopt the same traditional attitude when new sweeping changes are proposed by senior management: This, too, shall pass.

After the cost-reduction plan is approved, the next step is to develop milestone tasks associated with each cost-reduction recommendation. For example, consider a recommendation to "consolidate training functions in the field." An implementation plan should be developed for that recommendation as follows:

TASK: CONSOLIDATE TRAINING FUNCTIONS IN THE FIELD

Milestone	*Milestone Date*	*Responsibility*
Identify and catalog all field training functions	March 30	Training Manager
Identify the primary site for all training	April 16	Facility Manager
Gather all necessary equipment for training to the primary site	May 1	Facility Manager
Notify affected employees of the planned move or redeployment	May 1	Training Manager
Complete all logistical tasks and begin conducting training at the newly consolidated site	May 15	Training Manager

This implementation plan can then be combined with the implementation plans for all of the other recommendations to be implemented as part of the cost-reduction program. At the end of each month, all of the tasks due to be completed in that month should be reviewed in a senior executive meeting with a status report regarding whether the task was, in fact, accomplished and, if not, what steps are being taken to implement that task.

Generally, it's a good idea to designate a single employee with responsibility for the implementation of the cost-reduction plan. This employee (with support from other employees) would have responsibility for tasks such as working with managers to monitor and facilitate implementation, interpreting recommendations and milestone tasks, reporting implementation status and progress to senior managers, and tracking the actual savings that result from the cost-reduction plan.

Rebudgeting is also an important step at this point in the cost-reduction effort. The entire budget should be recast to reflect the projected cost savings that would result from the implementation of the cost-reduction program. The rebudgeting will solidify in the minds of company managers that the cost-reduction plan will, in fact, be implemented. Without such a rebudgeting, there would be little incentive for managers to achieve the savings projected for this program.

> To redeploy people in your organization, start at the top.

There will probably be fewer positions in your organization chart as a result of the cost-reduction program. The best way to fill those positions is to examine the newly-revised organization chart for your company and decide who will fill the top management positions. Those people decide who will fill the positions in the next level, and so on down the organization.

The intent is to allow the president of the organization, or the most senior salaried position in the company, to select his or her own subordinates. Those employees would then select their subordinates, and so on throughout the organization. To ensure that everyone in the organization gets a fair chance at all available positions, the company should actively encourage managers to look outside of their own departments to fill the positions beneath them.

At one company, the president took this process one step further than we had intended. After the board of directors approved the cost-reduction program, the incumbent president announced: "The employee selection process will now begin." He then offered the board his resignation and left the room to allow them to select a candidate for the presidency of the company.

The board selected the incumbent president to fill his own position, but the gesture made a very important point. Every position in the new organization chart was to be considered vacant. In reviewing the activities and functions performed by the organization, the cost-reduction study team did not evaluate the qualifications or merits of any individual employees; they simply determined whether the functions performed by each position were necessary to the overall effectiveness of the organization.

Therefore, just because an employee's position is eliminated doesn't mean that the employee should be eliminated. And, on the other hand, an employee whose position remains intact shouldn't necessarily be guaranteed that he or she will remain in that position. Throughout this selection process, all positions should be considered vacant until filled, and all employees should be considered candidates until selected.

It is likely that, after a cost-reduction program is implemented, there may not be enough positions in the organization to retain all of the employees working for that organization. Accordingly, the company has to consider redeployment options for those employees. Those options include attrition, early retirement, voluntary severance, and involuntary severance. Each of these complex options should be carefully considered in consultation with your human resource, legal, and financial experts for the implications for your organization.

Don't keep your employees in the dark.

It's usually next to impossible to keep reorganization plans quiet. And once word leaks out, what some employees don't know, they'll make up. Such rumors probably won't help your cost-reduction efforts. In fact, an atmosphere of openness and a willingness to communicate even unpleasant truths is far more likely to help maintain employee productivity levels and minimize anxiety and the sense of insecurity that usually accompanies the initiation of a major cost-reduction program.

This doesn't mean, however, that you should air every detail of your cost-reduction plan as it is being developed. Management cannot, and should not, make all of its decisions in a public forum. Instead, open communication simply means that the company should regularly supply accurate information about the cost-reduction program so that employees will understand why the program is being implemented and will know the schedule for implementation. Later, this communications effort should include helping employees comprehend how the cost-reduction program affects them and what their roles will be in the "new order."

Typically, questions during and immediately after the cost-reduction effort include:

- How will the cost-reduction program affect union negotiations or the union agreement?

- How will equal employment opportunity or affirmative action be taken into account in any work force reductions?

- Will there be a hiring freeze? (Or, alternatively, why are some departments hiring people from the outside when we are probably about to reduce the number of people working here?)

- Will these cost reductions make us more competitive?

- How did the decision to undergo a cost-reduction program occur?

- Will our planned salary increases be affected by the cost-reduction program?

- Doesn't the fact that we're going through this massive cost-reduction program mean that senior management has done a bad job of running the company in the past? Are any senior executives going to be fired as a result?

One of the most important concepts that must be communicated—not only to employees, but to customers, stockholders, and other interested groups—is what the company will not be doing anymore. If you've eliminated some of the activities that your company was performing, you've probably eliminated something that some customer somewhere really likes. By telling that customer in advance why that activity will be eliminated, and by demonstrating that the elimination will result in a reduced cost for your product or service, the company can mitigate or even reverse some of the public relations damage that could result.

When one West Coast electric and gas utility shut down several of its remote field offices, its chairman and president made several trips to the local media and town councils to explain why the decision was made. As a result, some of the local papers paid tribute to the company in editorials commending it for taking steps to reduce costs.

Employees particularly need to recognize that some things will no longer be done. Some employees will find that their jobs have changed significantly and may in a few cases be totally different from their previous jobs. But, in the absence of clear and repeated communications from management, your employees will attempt to perform their old and new jobs simultaneously. They considered their old jobs to be important, and—notwithstanding any decision from senior management not to perform those jobs anymore—will probably try to continue to perform them, with burnout and frustration resulting. Accordingly, your company should revise position descriptions and clearly communicate to affected employees how their position has changed and what old work will no longer be performed.

Not only is it helpful to communicate freely, it is often beneficial to repeat the same messages several times. Where a major cost-reduction program results in extensive reorganization, employee reaction is likely to follow a well-documented pattern found in all major psychological adjustments: Shock, defensive retreat, acknowledgment, and acceptance. As employees pass through each of these stages, you should reiterate your company's plans and goals, reminding employees that certain things will remain constant. Equally important is bringing home the reality of the impending reorganization so that employees have the time they need to plan their futures.

> Once you've been through a massive cost-reduction
> program, you will vow never to go through another
> one again. Ever!

Cost-reduction programs, particularly those that result in layoffs, are painful. Morale is low, anxiety is high, there is a period of "mourning" following the layoffs for those who have "departed." Under these circumstances, it is difficult to bring operations back to normal again. But, as in any challenge, there is opportunity. You now have a work force that will dedicate itself to avoiding such dramatic changes in the future.

Now is the time to harness that energy and redirect the organization in a positive effort toward greater competitiveness and cost-effectiveness.

Several companies have taken advantage of this rare opportunity not only to reorganize and streamline the company, but also to establish firmly the mission and shared values of the organization. They also work to avoid the mistake, common in such restructurings, of ignoring the "survivors"—the remaining employees.

At one company, a separate company team was set up. It consisted of seven highly qualified company employees charged with identifying the current corporate culture and then developing the appropriate mechanisms to change that culture to meet the needs of the future.

The team members conducted extensive interviews of the board of directors and senior management, reviewed literature, and interviewed utility and nonutility companies that had successfully instilled in their employees a culture that met competitive and other business requirements. As a result, an overall corporate mission statement was prepared and put before all employees. The company also established four new goals that were consistent with the necessary redirection of the company.

The team members found substantial evidence that, with both employees and its customers, the company had done a good job of instilling a culture that emphasized quality service and a quality product. Accordingly, the company embraced two goals related to its product and service to show that it intended to retain those values, even after the cost-reduction effort:

- "We will add value to our products through a strong service orientation that is responsive to customer and shareholder needs.

- "We will provide price and quality options that are responsive to customer requirements."

The company also found, however, that it needed to change significantly two major aspects of its culture. The utility hadn't done as well as it could have in rewarding employees based on performance or in placing emphasis on controlling costs. As a result, the company developed two additional financial and employee goals to change the corporate mindset in these areas:

- "We will be price-competitive, and our prices— adjusted for inflation—will not increase over time. Our costs, adjusted for inflation, will decrease over time, thereby maximizing the profitability that we share with our customers and stockholders.

- "We will provide an atmosphere where all employees contribute to their maximum potential and ability, and are rewarded based on demonstrated performance."

All of these goals were accompanied by systematic changes throughout the company in its processes and procedures, such as budgeting and compensation. As these changes were made, they reinforced in the minds of employees and managers that the organization was different now, representing a mix of traditional values and new ideas.

There is no question that the process of cost reduction can be painful and often difficult. But it has its rewards. Many of the companies that have conducted such cost-reduction programs have been able to save money for their customers, make money for their shareholders, and avoid being whipsawed by dramatic changes in their business and economic environments.

Perhaps most important, the companies that go through this process end up with a work force that is highly motivated to avoid such traumatic organizational changes in the future. In order to prevent such cost-reduction programs from recurring, however, the company should, at this point, take steps to build cost control into its day-to-day business operations.

Part Two
Cost Control

8
Cost Control

Cost control is the art of maintaining a lean and cost-effective organization.

Remember the diet analogy we used earlier? We said that cost reduction was like going on a diet, while cost control was like staying in shape.

Because weight control is such an agonizing and personal lifelong struggle, I can only smile sadly when I see many companies attempt to bring down and control their costs. The symptoms are familiar and painful: The slow and agonizing process of layoffs and cost reductions, traumatic psychological adjustment as the organization becomes thinner and more streamlined, triumph when the cost-reduction goal has been achieved, and satisfaction when the newly-

114

slimmed organization starts attracting more customers because of its reduced prices.

Then, with that success in the market, comes more profit and more money to spend. Company managers start coming up with new and innovative ways to spend that money, and senior executives, flush with cash and eager for the approval of subordinates and others in the organization, slowly but steadily allow more and more such expenditures. The company once again becomes bloated and misshapen, prices start rising, and its customers begin to turn away.

And before you know it, it's time for yet another diet.

Cost-effectiveness, like weight control, is not a one-shot operation. It represents a lifelong commitment to ensuring that high quality customer service is provided at the lowest possible cost.

Cost control is particularly difficult because, unlike cost reduction, there is no short-term goal to aim for and no end in sight. The process must be built into everything that company managers and employees do. It is a matter of continuing self-discipline, and must be reinforced constantly without the opportunity to reach a single target or end point.

Unfortunately, it is also counter to everything that we have trained managers and employees to do over the past several decades. And it will take a revolution in business systems to retrain employees to think in terms of cost-effectiveness.

> Managers (at their worst) like to add staff, spend money, and build empires; and (at their best) like to devote as many resources as possible to satisfying the customer. Both are contrary to effective cost control.

In most organizations, almost every internal system is geared toward rewarding employees for spending the company's money. For example, in the typical organization:

- The budgeting system is generally based on how much you've already spent and rewards you for spending a lot of money. If you budgeted $5,000,000 for your department last year and actually spent $7,000,000 without being blatantly wasteful, chances are your company's management will budget $6,000,000 for you in the coming year—and will congratulate themselves on "restraining" your spending. On the other hand, if you restrained yourself, and spent only $3,000,000 of your budgeted $5,000,000 for the year, you probably will be punished by having your budget slashed for the upcoming year.

- The compensation system is based, at least in part, on the number of employees and the size of the budget you manage. The more money you spend, the more you make!

- Services that are shared throughout the organization (such as data processing, information systems development, and legal services) are provided at no cost to each department, thereby encouraging their maximum use, regardless of the expense entailed.

- The human resource system hires, promotes, and transfers employees with little regard to the past spending practices of the employee.

- The performance measurement system is based on the achievement of goals irrespective of costs. If the goal for you or your department is to keep the customer satisfaction rate at a 98 percent level or higher, or to make sure that customer telephone calls are answered within three rings, you will pour as many resources into your activities as it takes to meet those goals.

Not that customer satisfaction isn't an important goal; in fact, it is the single most important goal for any organization. But how about looking at the cost/benefit tradeoffs? Would your customers be willing to wait longer on the telephone for their calls to be answered, if it would shave the price of your product?

Remember: Providing your customer with the highest quality product at the lowest possible price is the ultimate customer service.

Even when organizations do take steps to control costs, those steps can be less than effective. At many organizations, for example, there is a reward system in place for cost-reduction suggestions. Employees who identify opportunities to control expenses generally receive small cash prizes or gifts. Often, however, the prizes or gifts are so small as to be almost inconsequential, and the reward program becomes a joke.

Even worse, many companies publicly reward and praise their employees for coming up with important cost-reduction suggestions—and then do little to ensure that those suggestions are implemented. The feeling throughout the whole organization is that the reward system is a farce, and that the company isn't really serious about controlling costs.

The major problem with such reward programs is that they treat cost-reduction ideas as something special, rather than an expected requirement in the job of each and every employee. With those programs in place, the employee tends to feel that doing business as usual is the norm, while thinking about the job and coming up with improvements is unique and unexpected and deserves a special reward.

In order to effectively implement a cost-control mentality, the concept of cost control must be integrated into every business system in the company.

> Cost control consists of asking many of the same questions as in cost reduction—but answering them continuously.

In order to implement a long-term cost-control program effectively, an organization must address the following questions:

- *What do we do and why?* This involves setting a clear direction for the organization through a formal strategic planning process—the single most important step in a cost-control program.

- *How much does it cost us to do it?* The cost-effective organization uses "strategic budgeting" to answer this question: A system of budgeting that ties the dollars spent by the organization to the goals and objectives as set forth in its strategic plan.

- *How can we encourage executives and managers to reduce costs?* Cost-effectiveness requires that executives and managers understand the full costs of their activities and take steps continually to reduce those costs.

• *How do we change the culture and environment of the entire organization to encourage ongoing cost reduction?* This involves building cost control into clear goals and objectives for each and every employee.

These questions are translated into a flow chart on the following page. Notice that this flow chart differs from the cost-reduction flow chart shown earlier in one respect: This cost-control flow chart is made up of "ripples" back and forth between the first and last points; that is, cost control is a continuous feedback process with the results of one program modifying and changing another, which in turn modifies another, and so on. It is a process that never stops, that is dynamic, and reaches no clear endpoint, except that it results in a streamlined and effective organization that never loses its competitiveness.

Cost control is a "continuous feedback loop." It is an ongoing process that reaches no clear endpoint, and must be constantly monitored and reinforced.

Approach to Cost Control

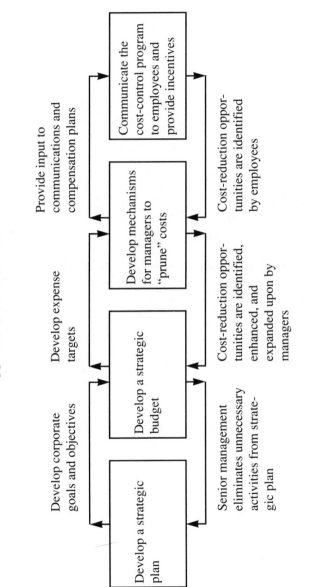

Develop corporate goals and objectives

Develop expense targets

Provide input to communications and compensation plans

Develop a strategic plan

Develop a strategic budget

Develop mechanisms for managers to "prune" costs

Communicate the cost-control program to employees and provide incentives

Senior management eliminates unnecessary activities from strategic plan

Cost-reduction opportunities are identified, enhanced, and expanded upon by managers

Cost-reduction opportunities are identified by employees

9

Strategic Planning
(What Are We Doing and Why?)

> Before you can find the cheapest air fare, you first
> have to figure out where you're going.

Beautiful new television sets, microwave ovens, and
other household appliances shined as they sat on dozens of
shelves in a storefront in the downtown area. Shoppers
roamed the halls, impressed with the merchandise, talking
to sales representatives, even signing a contract for some of
the electronic gadgets and arranging for their delivery. The
store had all the outward signs of a bustling and highly successful home appliance retail outlet.

There was only one hitch. The company running this
store was not in the retail sales or home appliance business.

The appliance store was an outgrowth of the company's main function, which was sales of energy and fuel. And a look at the company's financial statements emphasized that this appliance store was well beyond the mainstream of the company's expertise.

No one in the organization knew much about retail credit card sales, consumer financing, or point-of-sale marketing. As a result, the company lost significant amounts of money on both the sale and the service of home appliances. Except for the incredible profit margins on the extended warranties that it offered to its customers, there would have been substantial losses for the home appliance sales operation in all of the previous five years.

Unfortunately, this company was operating without a strategic plan. Without such a plan, there was no systematic way for the company to determine whether its money was being invested in a cost-effective manner. When they ultimately did perform a quick review of the market, its customers, and the competition, the company determined that the chances that its home appliance division would ever be successful were slim.

And so the company shut down its little home appliance store, a burden to the many customers who had been taking advantage of some of the outrageously low prices offered by the store, but a great relief to all of the company's stockholders.

Without an understanding of the company's strategic plan—the direction in which the company is headed, and the mechanisms by which it proposes to get there—employees simply cannot operate in a cost-effective manner. Managers and employees face economic tradeoffs almost every day. If senior executives have not provided general guidance as to the relative value of providing additional service to the customer versus providing additional share value to the company's stockholders, all of the company managers are likely to make decisions based on their best guess regarding the tradeoffs between those two factors.

And the greater the number of employees in your organizations, the greater the number of different outcomes that are likely to occur. As a result, the chaos gets worse as the company gets larger.

There are several instances where planning becomes a major issue in cost control. It is particularly important when the organization:

- *Has no coherent strategic plan.* Without a plan, companies can blunder into some strange and incompatible business areas—like the energy company that stumbled into appliance sales.

- *Has a strategic plan that conflicts with reality.* One company had a strategic plan that called for high growth, and consequently staffed up their manufacturing plant to meet the projected demand for their product. However, when a senior management team checked their projections with those of local economists and university professors, they found that their projections were wildly optimistic. By revising their plan assumptions downward, the company was able to control manufacturing costs significantly.

• *Has a coherent and realistic plan, but doesn't follow it.* For example, if the primary mission of the company is to "provide low-cost and reliable automobile parts sales and service," it is reasonable to question whether having a video department that produces commercials for other companies furthers that mission.

The first step in providing uniform guidelines to determine what services should be performed (and what shouldn't) is the development of a coherent and realistic strategic plan. The strategic plan spells out in considerable detail the general mission of the company and the specific goals and objectives that the company expects to reach in achieving that mission.

> The mission statement is the foundation for your company's strategic plan.

The mission statement is a brief statement of the purpose and ultimate goal of the company. It can be as short as one sentence, and certainly should be no longer than one paragraph. As a general rule, the mission statement should be short enough that your company's chief executive officer can recite it while standing on one foot.

Some corporate mission statements can almost be engraved on the head of a pin. One large company has as its mission statement the simple and initially enigmatic slogan, "Top 5 in 5." The mission is widely publicized throughout the company, and its meaning is clear to all employees: The organization intends to become one of the top five companies in its industry within five years.

Given the fact that senior management and the company's employees already have a good idea of what the organization does and what it intends to achieve, a draft mission statement should be easy to develop and present to senior executives and board members for further discussion. Some examples are:

Type of Company	Mission Statement
Health Insurance	"Our mission is to promote maximum access to an affordable, stable, and effective health-care financing and delivery system in our service territory."
Electric and Water Utility	"Our purpose is to be the low-cost supplier among our competitors of high-value energy and water services."
Marketing Organization	"Our role is to acquire new and profitable customers."

A draft mission statement then should be discussed and debated among senior executives and board members before being finalized. Don't be surprised if the development of such a statement creates controversy and long periods of heated discussion. If the mission has not been clearly or formally articulated before, it can be surprising how many different goals and objectives have been informally developed for the organization by its employees. The process of developing a formal mission statement has taken months at some companies.

Development of the mission statement is both a quantitative and a qualitative process. It requires a clear understanding of the economics of the activities being performed by the organization and the market for its services. This is a largely quantitative function, which involves calculating internal rates of return for the products and services currently provided by the organization as well as projections of future demand for those products and services.

But it also entails a qualitative assessment of the market, including the company's own strengths and weaknesses. After all, your company's mission statement probably should not be as broad as, "To conduct any and all legal activities that result in an internal rate of return greater than 11 percent and show a significant market growth potential" (unless you're a venture capital firm).

The mission statement, when fully developed, is important for what it does not say as well as for what it says. A health insurance company may not be in the business of providing automobile or life insurance. An electric and water utility may not want to be in the business of providing telephone, cable television, or natural gas services. A marketing organization may want to focus its attention on new customers, leaving to others the work of selling products to existing customers.

Therefore, simply by developing a mission statement, the company may be able to eliminate some activities that are not related to the primary purpose of the company. Many companies have reduced costs at this stage of the process: Department stores have eliminated their insurance sales functions, computer manufacturing companies have ended their forays into office supplies, and restaurant chains have discontinued their retail grocery outlets. Each change resulted in reduced costs and improved profitability, but only because the mission statement, as finally developed, combined realistic quantitative financial and economic assessment with the senior management's own inherent knowledge of the company and its market.

Once the mission statement is developed, however, the company should establish the goals and objectives that are related to that mission.

The mission statement should be broken down into a series of goals, and then further broken down into objectives, and then further into tasks, so that each and every activity in the organization is directly related to the company's mission statement.

In order to determine the goals and objectives that should be incorporated in the strategic plan, the company should answer such questions as: What factors (both positive and negative) differentiate us from other companies in the market? Where can we improve most? How can we build on our strengths? Where do we spend the most money, and how can those costs be minimized? These questions can then lead to a strategic plan that builds upon strengths while correcting weaknesses, thus making the company even more profitable and allowing it to be run in a cost-effective manner. Let's see how this works in practice.

One financial services company conducted a comprehensive review of its own activities and commercial success. The company, while certainly successful, had become stagnant in both its financial performance and in terms of its image in the market. After considering the results of this review, the company established the following mission statement: "We want to become the premier financial services company in our service territory as measured by market share and profitability."

To that end, the company developed the following goals:

• Improve market share

• Improve the internal financial strength of the company

• Improve the company's image through a comprehensive customer and community relations program

• Attract and retain high-caliber personnel

Each of these long-term goals was then associated with a set of short-term goals; for example, the goal of "improve market share" had the following four-year quantitative objectives:

	Current Market Share	Projected Market Share: Next Four Years			
		Year 1	Year 2	Year 3	Year 4
State	38.2	39	40	41	42
National	18.5	19	19	20	21

The company recognized that it had to provide more than mere numbers for the organization to shoot for. It also had to establish a "roadmap" of activities for the organization to follow in achieving these quantitative goals. Accordingly, it developed qualitative objectives that could be readily translated into specific activities. For example, the goal of "improve market share" also had the following specific qualitative objectives:

- Develop competitive products by carefully examining the needs of our customers and the products developed by our competitors

- Develop marketing channels and networks to support new and existing products

- Establish new marketing contacts and build on existing contacts to sell new and existing products

These tasks were then linked to different quantitative goals, such as establishing new market contacts and building on existing contacts to sell new and existing products:

	Current Activity	Projected Activity: Next Four Years			
		Year 1	Year 2	Year 3	Year 4
Contacts	400	425	450	475	500
Sales	200	225	275	290	300

In other words, in order to meet the goals for increased state and national market share, the company has to significantly increase the number of contacts and sales it makes over the next four years.

The plan looked good and complete to the company at this point, but there was one more step before the plan could be finalized: It had to be "checked" against the actual activities of the organization.

> Employee participation should serve as a checkpoint for the completeness and accuracy of your strategic plan.

After these qualitative goals were developed, each person in the company was required to identify his or her activities for the following year, keying them to each of the goals of the company. For example, the financial services company gave its employees a list of all the qualitative objectives of the organization, numbered as follows (to show an abbreviated example):

1. Maintain and improve market share

   a. Develop competitive products by carefully examining the needs of our customers and the products being developed by our competitors

b. Develop marketing channels and networks to support new and existing products

c. Establish new marketing contacts and build on existing contacts to sell new and existing products

2. Improve the internal financial strength of the company

   a. Monitor and analyze the financial performance of the company

   b. Explore alternative financing mechanisms

   c. Manage the company's near-term downsizing and continue to identify cost-reduction opportunities

Based on this list, the employees were then asked to list all of their activities, accounting for one hundred percent of their time relative to these goals. An example of the form used for this analysis is as follows:

Objective	Task	Percent of Time Spent on Task
1a. Develop competitive products	Develop health and life insurance for specialized market segments	50%
1c. Establish new marketing contacts	Contact 40 new customers	40%
2a. Monitor financial performance	Prepare sales projections for next year	10%
TOTAL (Must equal 100%)		100%

The following definitions apply to this form:

Objective: One of the objectives of the organization as shown in its strategic plan

Task: The specific task performed by the employee taking the survey

Percent of time spent on task: The percent of time that the employee projects spending on this task over the next twelve months

The example shown above is abbreviated. Most employees will have far more tasks shown but should be encouraged to lump similar tasks together so that they total no less than five to ten percent of their total time.

If your company chooses not to involve all employees, or if certain employees cannot be effectively surveyed for this purpose, managers can estimate the amount of time spent by their departments on each task. But involving as many employees as possible in this process improves the accuracy of the information as well as encourages employees to become involved in and recognize the importance of the strategic planning process.

After all employees provide their input, this information—particularly if it is computerized, even using a simple personal computer spreadsheet program—can provide valuable information as part of the planning process. After such surveys, companies have been able to identify activities that were not part of the corporate plan and that therefore should be eliminated, or they have modified their corporate plan to reflect activities that were forgotten in the initial planning process.

The written data should be collated and reviewed before the corporate plan is finalized. There may be activities that are being performed by your organization that were not included in any part of the plan, and that should either be (a) incorporated in the plan, or (b) eliminated.

When this survey is concluded, the company has a plan that provides a basic mission for the entire organization, a set of corporate goals and objectives, and a work force that fully understands its role in achieving those goals and objectives. The next step is to ensure that the resources that the company dedicates to those goals and objectives are appropriate, and costs throughout the organization associated with unnecessary activities are eliminated.

> "Benchmarking" can be a useful tool in developing your strategic plan. But done incorrectly, it can have your company racing for a second-place finish.

Benchmarking is the process of examining performance in other industries similar to your own, and then setting the targets in your strategic plan to meet or exceed that performance.

Your strategic plan, to be successful, must incorporate analysis of your market. That includes looking at your current market share, projecting the future trend in that share, examining your internal return or profitability on your business lines, and determining how best to allocate your resources.

One key aspect of your market that cannot be ignored is your competition. If you are doing well in a given market and your competition is doing well, you are probably wise to remain in that line of business. If you and your competitors are both doing poorly, it might be smarter to reduce or eliminate your investment in that market. If you are doing well in an area where your competition is doing poorly, you have a clear market strength. Your plan should build on that strength.

Perhaps most important, if you are struggling in an area in which your competition appears to be doing well, it is critical to understand why your competition is doing so much better and to take steps to improve your own performance if you are to remain in that line of business.

For example, one of the goals of our financial services company was to make 425 marketing contacts in the first year of the plan, increasing that to 500 by the fourth year. The company might then identify other companies, both inside and outside of the financial services industry, to determine how many contacts per representative they expect to make and how they intend to improve that performance in the coming years. By applying those statistics to the actual and projected performance of their own company, the plan can incorporate realistic targets for marketing contacts, using the best tools and techniques employed by companies that appear to excel in these areas, and "stretch" targets, which attempt to exceed the best known industry performance.

Benchmarking generally involves identifying those companies (both within and outside your market area) that excel in the business areas that you have decided are important to your company and then assigning one or more company employees to learn the tools and techniques employed by those companies. Some methods that are often used to learn about other companies include:

- Published documents, such as annual reports and other documents published by the company, filings to the Securities and Exchange Commission, filings to other relevant government agencies (for example, gas, electric, water, and telephone utilities often have to supply much information to the utility regulatory commission that would be considered highly confidential by nonregulated companies), newspaper articles and publications, and the reports of financial analysts. Particularly useful are the reports of credit agencies such as Dun and Bradstreet, which can provide good information on the profitability of companies with lines of business similar to those you are in or considering.

- Direct contact with the companies. To the extent that the company you are interested in is not in direct competition, they may be willing to share their tools, tricks, and techniques with you. One electric utility performed a benchmarking analysis involving, among others, an airline and an overnight courier service. Both the airline and the courier service were very forthcoming about their processes and procedures, and a number of long-term information-sharing relationships developed between the utility and their nonutility colleagues.

Although benchmarking is an important tool in strategic analysis, it can be misused. You can easily wind up institutionalizing a "catch-up" philosophy. That is, if you continually teach your employees that the driving force behind your organization is to do as well as the competition, how will you ever wind up doing better?

Good benchmarking compensates for this problem by setting several targets that "leapfrog" the competition and that aim to exceed the best practices of other companies in the industry according to a predetermined schedule. But even that has a drawback: Your competition does not intend to stagnate.

For example, if you develop your strategic plan this year, you may find during your benchmarking process that your primary competitor sells 500,000 shoetrees per year. You then resolve that you will sell 700,000 shoetrees five years from now, thereby "leapfrogging" ahead of your competitor in five years.

Five years from now, you meet your target of 700,000 shoetree sales. But you discover, to your horror, that your competitor now sells over 900,000 per year. Relative to your competitor, you have made no progress in your marketing effort.

Benchmarking is an important tool, but it shouldn't be the primary driver in your strategic plan. That should come from examining your internal skills, capabilities, and interests as well as looking at market potential. If you take full advantage of all of your assets and build your business based on a realistic assessment of financial possibilities and internal capabilities, soon you will be the best in your business. Then you can let other companies use *you* as *their* benchmark.

Without a strategic plan, you have no idea whether you're spending your money effectively or not.

There are companies today that have divisions that compete with each other, that operate unprofitably but continue to survive, or that operate with a tremendous potential for success with little recognition. There are manufacturing companies with full-service audio sound studios that are rented out to musicians and other users, real estate companies that operate florist and botany supply stores, and trade associations that operate consulting firms—with no evidence that these services are profitable, but having no strategic plan with which to argue that these services are beyond the scope of the organization.

More important from a cost-control perspective, if you are going to ask your employees to monitor costs continually and identify opportunities to reduce those costs, they first need to understand what the organization is attempting to achieve. Without such guidance, they can only suggest and implement cost control in a haphazard and sometimes inconsistent manner. With such guidance, however, all company employees can march on a single path toward cost-reduction opportunities.

Your senior management also benefits from a clear strategic plan. The budget and other management information they receive can be linked to the goals and objectives of the strategic plan, so that they can allocate resources in a reasonable way. The process that allows companies to link the strategic plan to their planned and actual expenditures is called "strategic budgeting"—and it represents one of the best opportunities to monitor costs and ensure that the organization operates in the most cost-effective manner possible.

10

Strategic Budgeting (How Much Do We Pay for What We Do?)

A "mystery budget"—a budget that is so complex and poorly written that it defies understanding—is not only fairly common in organizations, it is also the worst enemy that a cost-effective organization can have.

". . . and when this number gets above seven thousand," the manager of a customer service department once told us, "I really put pressure on my employees until it gets back down."

The manager was explaining his budget and pointed to a number labeled, in the cryptic manner typical of so many business budgets, "CLASS DEP OPT REV." Since this meant nothing to us, we asked what it meant.

"Well, I don't know what those words stand for," he replied, "but what I think it means is that the operating revenue . . . no, it's really a depreciation classification that has . . . um . . . well, I mean, it has some . . . department revenue that. . . ."

After a bit more of this stream of consciousness, he finally admitted: "Well, I'm not really sure exactly what it means. But," he added, "when it gets over seven thousand, my boss is unhappy, then I get unhappy, then I let my people know I'm unhappy, and we always manage to get it back down somehow."

An amazing number of the budgets being circulated in the business world are absolutely nonintelligible. And even those written in a reasonably clear manner often contribute little to an understanding of how money is being spent by the organization.

Sometimes companies that have gotten too comfortable with their current budget system lose sight of how useless it is as a tool for controlling costs and improving cost effectiveness within the company. Consider the following budget, which is the actual budget for a division of a large and successful business (except for changes designed to protect the identity of the company):

	Budgeted	Actual
Vice President's Office		
Salaries	35000	35000
Supplies	15000	14872
Office Equipment	3500	3741
General Distribution		
Salaries	375000	392000
Supplies	130000	127000
Office Equipment	7500	7905
Program Planning		
Salaries	724000	732000
Supplies	25000	24071
Office Equipment	2000	1112

When we talked to the vice president in charge of this division, we naturally had several questions:

- Does the vice president really make just $35,000 a year? (No, the vice president's salary is split among all three of the budget areas, including general distribution and program planning.)

- What are "General Distribution" and "Program Planning"? ("General Distribution" represents the work done by the manager of distribution and his staff; "Program Planning" is a catchall category that covers everything not in the vice president's office or General Distribution.)

- Why are salaries so high in "Program Planning"? (Because we've lumped all the secretarial and clerical personnel in that category.)

- What is the difference between "supplies" and "office equipment"? (It's a typographical error; the word "supplies" should be "suppliers," which means outside vendors such as law firms and contractors.)

- Is this budget, which is the companywide budget developed by the corporate finance department for use by all divisions, useful to you in running your division? (No. We use an informal spreadsheet program that we've developed ourselves on our personal computers to monitor and keep track of our budget.)

Imagine! There are plenty of companies that spend hundreds of thousands of dollars to develop a corporate budget for use by all employees throughout the company, and then those employees spend additional time and effort developing a different type of budget—using identical data—so that the information is more useful for their purposes. But as this actual example makes clear, many company budgets are simply unusable for day-to-day management.

More important than that, however, is that senior executives and the board of directors cannot possibly have a good understanding of the expenses of the business when the budget data is not understandable. How would you, as chairman or president of the company, even begin to get a handle on the expenses of a vice president who has ill-defined "General Distribution" and "Program Planning" functions?

Naturally, the absence of a clear budgeting system critically hampers the ability of any organization to maintain control of its costs on an ongoing basis and leads to creeping fat within the company. There are two steps that any company can take to improve the budgeting process thereby improving the handle it has on its expenses:

- Clean up the current budgeting system so that the information presented in it is clear, understandable, and can be readily reviewed and questioned by senior executives and the board of directors.

- Tie the budgeting process to the planning process so that every dollar spent by the organization is linked to a goal or objective that the company has developed ("strategic budgeting").

Each of these steps can greatly enhance your company's ability to get control of its expenses, improving its profitability and its competitiveness. But there is a substantial amount of work entailed in revamping the budgeting system in any organization, and it is important to make the right decisions and choices regarding the proper budgeting system as far in advance of the actual system development as possible.

> Your neighbor should be able to look at your budget and ask reasonably intelligent questions about your business.

Is your budget system in need of revamping, or does it provide information in a clear and reliable format to all interested parties? To find out, subject your budget to the following test:

- Ask your senior executives if their departments have developed their own independent budgets

- Ask middle level managers to explain the budget for their own departments—and then, as a sort of trick question, ask them to look at the budget for another relatively unfamiliar department and comment on that (with the understanding that there are no recriminations for "wrong" questions or answers)

- Ask a reasonably capable business executive from another (noncompeting) firm to review your budget and comment on it

- Examine your own questions and concerns about the budget and the information it contains

Budgeting represents a unique opportunity for companies to understand the activities performed by the entire company on a regular basis. And this is precisely why so many budgets are nonintelligible: Very often, senior officers—embarrassed at having to answer detailed questions about their own operations and spending patterns—subconsciously or deliberately conspire to develop corporate budgets that disguise meaningful spending patterns. Sometimes even the chief executive officer is involved in the plot in order to discourage unwanted probing by the board of directors.

The downside of this strategy, of course, is that it, in essence, encourages overspending by company managers. By preventing directors and executives from getting to the root cause of spending increases, the budget information limits the pressure on managers to reduce costs and streamline spending.

One way of improving the budgeting system is to conduct a comprehensive review of that system, getting opinions from those who use the budget information on a regular basis. If these company managers have developed their own informal budgeting systems in addition to the formal corporate system, find out what those informal budgets look like. How are they formatted, and what do they contribute to a better understanding of spending within that department? Are there common attributes or formats to the informal budgets throughout the company that can be incorporated into the corporate budget?

Creating a company task force that will work to improve the budget can result in enormous changes in the budgeting process, in the tracking of costs, and in the ability of the company to work cost-effectively. Such a task force should include participation in some form by representatives of the board of directors to ensure that the information they receive is meaningful.

There is another way to improve the budgeting system that requires a tremendous change in the way the budget is put together, and therefore requires a lot of work and psychological adjustment on the part of company managers. That is to think of the line items in the budgets in terms of their intended results rather than in terms of what the money is spent on.

For example, consider the case of a Washington-based lobbying organization. The organization had a somewhat confusing budget, but no more confusing than many of the budgets that businesses use. Like most budgets, it was an "item-based" budget, and each line represented specific items on which the organization was spending its money:

Example of an "Item-Based" Budget

Salaries	$1,250,000
Benefits	300,000
Outside Contractors:	
Law firms	500,000
Public relations firms	150,000
Management consultant	50,000
Travel	50,000
Office Supplies	15,000
Rent	300,000
Discretionary Fund	100,000
TOTAL BUDGET	$2,715,000

The organization could explain to its members and its board exactly how much was being spent on lawyers, airline tickets, and paper clips. But what those lawyers were doing, where they were going on those airplanes, and what papers were being clipped with those paper clips were a mystery that their "item-based" budget left unresolved.

After some confusion by its managers and members regarding the uses of its money, the organization recast this information into what it called a "strategic" budget. It projected what it needed to do to meet the goals and objectives stated in its strategic plan, and then budgeted appropriately (significantly altered to protect the identity of the company involved):

Example of a "Strategic" Budget

Propose and promote changes to the upcoming Dry Fish and Foul Act.....................................	$ 950,000
Prepare a court case challenging the constitutionality of the Clean Sidewalks regulations...	545,000
Analyze the economic impact of the proposed Scales and Weights amendments	400,000
Maintain contact with the White House and Congress to suggest nominations to the Iced Tea Review Board	350,000
Maintain ongoing contacts with White House and Congressional staff to determine issues of potential interest	300,000
Publish a book outlining the company's position on key legislative and regulatory issues.............	170,000
TOTAL BUDGET.................................	$2,715,000

Throughout the year, employees of this lobbying firm then filled out time sheets to determine how they were spending their time relative to these activities, and their salaries were allocated to budget areas based on the hours shown on those time sheets. Those costs were then compared to the amounts shown in the original budget.

When invoices came in, they were allocated to specific tasks. For example, when the law firm sent in its bill for work on the Clean Sidewalks lawsuit, the cost associated with that invoice was allocated to that line item of the budget.

For overhead expenses, such as office supplies or rent, each line item of the budget was assigned a certain percentage for overhead, so that those expenses were generally evenly distributed. (Although that wasn't always the case; for example, no rent or office supplies expenses were allocated to the Clean Sidewalks lawsuit, because that was being managed entirely by an outside law firm that used its own offices and supplies.)

What resulted from this type of budget? Senior executives and board members were able to examine the budget and to determine how resources were being allocated. They could ask intelligent questions that weren't immediately obvious from the item-based budget, such as:

- Is the Dry Fish and Foul Act really so important that it gets nearly twice as many dollars as anything else?

- Does it really cost $400,000 to do an economic analysis of the Scales and Weights amendments? Couldn't we hire an outside consulting firm or economics professor to do it more cheaply, and with more credibility?

- How many copies of our proposed book are we putting out, of what quality, and what benefits do we receive?

- Why do we care about who gets nominated to the Iced Tea Review Board?

Such questions enabled key customers and executives to steer the organization in the most useful direction and at the best possible price. "This has contributed enormously to my understanding of this company," one board member has said. "I feel for the first time like I fully understand everything that is going on."

How did company employees and managers react to this new system? Well, at first they hated it. It represented more paperwork (in the form of time sheets as well as in the budgeting process) and required more thought (this system doesn't lend itself well to simply increasing last year's budget by a certain percentage).

But this strategic budgeting process ultimately led many of those employees to identify and implement cost-reduction opportunities, as they continually questioned the need to perform certain activities in light of the issues that were deemed important by the organization. This was particularly true when they simply couldn't find "homes" in the budget for some of the activities that they were performing—and the company, after reviewing those activities, confirmed that those functions could be eliminated.

Could employees manipulate the system? Sure, employees can manipulate almost any budget system. They would sometimes deliberately misallocate funds, shifting expenses that should properly be allocated to an issue that was being squeezed for money over to an issue that had plenty of leftover funds.

Unlike the "item-based" budget, however, the strategic budget has an inherent checks-and-balances aspect that helps to uncover such misallocations. Each line item of the issue-based budget is supposed to produce results, and when those results aren't produced, questions are raised.

For example, some employees of the lobbying organization may discover, to their horror, that they are running $100,000 over budget on publishing and distributing their book. However, they also notice that they don't really need all of the funds appropriated for lobbying on the Clean Sidewalks amendments, because those amendments were voted down with unexpected ease early in the year. So the employees decide to allocate their book overrun to the Clean Sidewalks amendments, thereby coming in near budget on both issues.

Ah, but it doesn't work that way. At the end of the year (or perhaps before), the board and senior executives are likely to question why so much money was spent on the Clean Sidewalks issue when it appeared to be handled so easily. Then the company managers are in for some difficult questions, without any good answers except for one that starts: "Well, we ran over on expenses for the book publication, and we noticed that we had some money left over for Clean Sidewalks, so we. . . ."

Unlike the item-based budget, those responsible for reviewing the issue-based budget can make a quick assessment to determine whether the results achieved during the year justify the expenses incurred.

But what if priorities legitimately shift during the year? For example, what if no vacancies develop on the Iced Tea Review Board during the year (thus making it a much lower priority than the organization had envisioned at the beginning of the budget year), but Congress unexpectedly starts making changes to the all-important Law of the Sea Monkeys Treaty? The organization would have to shift funds, creating a new budget category for this unexpected new issue. And the board of directors and senior executives would be fully apprised, through the budgeting process, of this shift in the organization's priorities.

One note of caution: If you do choose to develop the strategic budget, it will have to be run in parallel with the item-based budget. After all, there will be times when you have to identify how much you are spending in total on salaries, or benefits, or travel. But the issue-based budget should be the primary budget, and should be circulated most widely and discussed most commonly among company managers.

How do you identify the issues in your strategic budget? If you have developed a strategic plan, the budget can be linked to each of the tasks you have already developed as goals and objectives for that plan.

> You can combine the development of your strategic plan with the development of your strategic budget.

Remember that, in developing your strategic plan, you set out qualitative objectives that described the tasks that you expected your organization to complete. Those tasks can serve as the line items in your strategic budget.

Moreover, in the process of establishing a strategic plan, you surveyed all of your employees to determine what tasks they performed and how those tasks related to the objectives of the organization. Your employees or their managers could elaborate on those tasks by providing additional information.

Your budget can be set up by having managers fill out forms like the following, which directly relate to the strategic planning information they've already developed:

TASK	Develop a new form of life and health insurance for selected markets
GOAL	2a. Develop and create new products
LABOR COST	2000 hours of a senior analyst (Grade 12) 250 hours of clerical support (Grade 3)
NONLABOR COST	$25,000 for a marketing consultant $35,000 for product testing
RESULTS	Sales of 300 new insurance policies by year-end

Definitions of the terms used in the form are as follows:

Task: The specific job to be performed by the employee or department

Goal: The related goal as stated in the organization's strategic plan, along with the number from the numbering system used in the plan for easy identification

Labor Cost: The number of hours required to perform the task and the grade levels of those performing the task (a standard formula can be applied to convert these figures into dollars for budgeting purposes)

Nonlabor Cost: Any out-of-pocket expenses related to performing the task

Results: The quantitative goal as articulated in the strategic plan as well as any other benefits that will be derived from performing this task.

If each of your managers presents forms such as these to the department responsible for budgeting, the forms can be converted to an issues-based corporate budget, with overhead factors calculated based on a predetermined allocation formula.

Preparation of such budget worksheets allows your managers to think about what they are doing and how each activity is linked to the overall strategy and direction of the corporation. Where activities are not directly linked, there is the possibility that an activity was inadvertently omitted from the plan, and that situation should be remedied. But if there is no logical reason for that activity to be conducted, it should be eliminated.

At an organization that performed this kind of planning review, one employee struggled endlessly to justify the hours that were spent re-reviewing financial statements that had already been reviewed by another department more properly suited to the task. The result: the employee, realizing the struggle was fruitless, finally eliminated the activity—although not without some choice criticisms of the whole strategic planning and budgeting process. (I know this employee's struggle was long, frustrating, agonizing, and ultimately fruitless, because *I* was that employee. And believe me, at that time I never thought I'd advocate strategic planning or budgeting for any other organization.)

Despite the concerns and complaints that you'll hear, particularly in the early stages of this process, a strategic planning and budgeting process ultimately benefits the company's board, customers, executives, and all of its employees.

> Periodically "zero base" your strategic plan and budget.

Generally speaking, you should keep your organization on the same strategic path for several years in order to avoid being whipsawed by annual or semiannual changes in direction. But periodically—generally every four or five years—your organization should "zero base" its strategy and budget to ensure that it fully reflects the business and market environment.

Zero-based budgeting became something of a business fad in the late 1970s. Its roots were in the presidency of Jimmy Carter, who had used zero-based budgeting while governor of Georgia, praised the methodology, and expressed the desire to implement a similar mechanism for the federal government.

Though difficult to achieve on a federal level, several organizations periodically zero base their activities successfully. "Zero basing" means to start from scratch; that is, to pretend that your organization has no strategic plan or budget and to develop one from ground zero.

Zero basing the strategic plan and budget involves a comprehensive review of the organization and environment and includes:

- A systematic review of the activities and market share trends of competitors

- Surveys of customers and potential customers to determine their desires and satisfaction level with the services and products provided by your organization and its competitors

- Complete listing of all activities that are performed or could be performed by your organization.

In short, it combines intensive elements of both cost-reduction and cost-control mechanisms.

Based on information received from the competitive analysis and customer surveys, the company then should sift through the activities and potential activities of the organization, prioritizing each, and performing those activities with the highest priority, given the limits on resources for the company.

In other words, zero basing the company involves a comprehensive replanning and rebudgeting effort.

This is not the sort of activity that your organization can put itself through on a yearly basis. In fact, some organizations stagger the responsibility, requiring separate departments to zero base their activities on different schedules. But the end result should be an intensive periodic review of the company's direction to determine whether significant changes in the economy, environment, or internal capabilities of the company should result in a major redirection of the organization.

Linking the budget to the company's strategic direction allows the company to ensure, on an ongoing basis, that the activities being performed by the organization are necessary, important, and contribute to the satisfaction of the customer and consequently to the profitability of the organization. Now, employees and managers must be encouraged and rewarded for their ongoing efforts to maintain a cost-effective organization. And this, too, requires a rethinking and rebuilding of some of the fundamental processes inherent in your organization.

11

"Pruning"
(How Do We Encourage Managers and Executives to Control Costs?)

> Corporate expenses, like trees, should be pruned around the edges on a regular basis.

A few years ago, we provided consulting support to a large energy company undergoing a massive downsizing and cost-reduction program. The program resulted in a substantial decrease in expenses and streamlining of the organization.

I met one of the vice presidents of that company in an airport recently. We talked briefly between flights, and he laughed when we discussed our earlier work for his organization. "You guys really missed a big opportunity in our department," the vice president grinned. "We use our own people for our wholesale distribution, and we could probably franchise or contract out that function at a tremendous cost savings to the company."

Expressing regret that we had missed the chance to reduce costs even further in his organization, I asked if he had later chosen to implement this change. "No," he replied, "we still use our own people." When I asked if he could still save money by franchising or contracting the wholesaling function, he said, "Probably." When I asked why he hadn't done it, he paused for a moment.

"Why should I?" he finally asked.

Good question.

When officers or managers in your organization have hundreds of full-time employees working for them, what incentive do they have for suggesting that their empire be eliminated? Particularly when, as in this case, their empire could be replaced with dozens of screaming and demanding franchisees.

Far better to retain the power and control that comes with supervising a large number of full-time employees. In most organizations, large departments not only mean greater prestige and more authority, but larger salaries and bonuses as well.

Sure, a strategic planning and budgeting process can help examine the big picture in your organization and identify key activities that could be done more effectively or not at all. But company managers need to be actively involved in the day-to-day process of cost control, identifying the myriad of smaller cost-reduction opportunities that continue to develop—all the while being assured that their power and authority will increase, rather than decline, as such opportunities are fully explored.

This is particularly true as concepts such as automation and contract labor for white collar functions become increasingly developed, allowing even more potential for cost reduction and cost control.

Companies that successfully implement cost-control mechanisms on a regular basis provide incentives to reduce costs in the following ways:

- Incorporating cost-reduction issues into regular management and employee meetings to encourage discussion of opportunities

- Implementing mechanisms to monitor cost-reduction and cost-control activities

- Developing chargeback systems to ensure that managers recognize the cost of corporate services

Some organizations refer to it as "pruning." Managers must continually prune costs, trimming expenses on an ongoing basis wherever opportunities can be found.

By implementing such an ongoing "pruning" mechanism—and by communicating and publicizing it widely throughout the organization—your company will take important steps to let employees, stockholders, and customers know that cost control is an ongoing process and not simply a one-time effort.

> Often, the best way to identify cost-reduction opportunities within one of your departments is to ask someone in another department.

One chief executive has been highly successful in getting his officers to "rat" on each other.

It occurred at the regular Friday morning meeting of all officers. There was always an item on the agenda to discuss corporate expenses and to pursue opportunities to reduce them. The chief executive officer used all the tricks he could think of—including badgering, pleading, and rewarding—to get his officers to come up with creative new ideas to prune costs.

Initially, his concept of this process was that he would get each officer to identify cost-reduction opportunities in his or her own area. And, at first, that is exactly what happened. But the process was slow and yielded relatively few nuggets.

Then the CEO had a brainstorm: At one meeting, during a discussion of the human resource process in the corporation, he turned to the Vice President of Engineering and said, "You've always complained that the hiring and recruiting process is too difficult in this company. What would you do if you were Vice President of Human Resources, to streamline that process?" The Vice President of Engineering, although one of the least shy of the officers, was initially hesitant about saying anything that might resemble a criticism of another officer. But soon ideas started pouring forth, first from the Vice President of Engineering, and then from others—ideas that ultimately contributed to effectively streamlining several human resource processes.

It helped that the Vice President of Human Resources was a good listener who didn't take the criticism personally. By responding well and actually implementing many of the recommendations that resulted from that meeting, that vice president helped establish a precedent for future similar discussions.

Thereafter, the agenda for each meeting included the processes and procedures for a given department. At one meeting the group discussed activities within the information systems department, and at the next they discussed purchasing and warehousing functions. Each of these discussions resulted in valuable changes in the company, and these changes almost invariably resulted in reduced costs for the organization.

Of course, each of the officers was also expected to explore cost-control opportunities in their own departments as well. But the process of looking at other departments and identifying cost-control opportunities from an outsider or user perspective, provided several advantages to the organization; for example, it:

- Allowed department managers to benefit from a fresh look at their organizations. Often, functions that they thought were useful to other departments turned out not to be valuable and were eliminated.

- Improved the quality of other discussions in the officers' meetings, allowing the officers to speak fully and frankly on a wide range of issues without fear of offending others.

- Encouraged the officers—who could often become isolated within their own departments and could develop "tunnel vision"—to learn about the inner workings and functions of other departments, thereby causing them to look at the broader picture and think organizationally rather than departmentally.

It can be tricky to encourage such discussions without having them degenerate into a shouting match with hurt feelings and resulting poor morale. The discussions have to be framed positively, and any attempt to sling arrows or mud should be shot down immediately.

On the other hand, such discussions cannot become love fests, with each officer tacitly agreeing to suggest minor changes to other departments in exchange for the right to be left alone when it comes time for their own processes and procedures to be reviewed.

The discussions must result in concrete action with rewards and recognition to the implementing department for controlling costs, and few recriminations (except where very clearly required) for past wasteful spending. And the entire officer group should see the results of their suggestions in their regular report of expenses. In other words, the discussions of cost-control opportunities must be actively managed by the chief executive officer or other person in charge of the meeting.

Such meetings do not have to be limited to officers. Lower-level employees can often participate in such meetings. To some extent such meetings do take place at many companies in the form of quality improvement. These meetings, often called "Quality Circles," involve both makers and users of company products and services. Although the primary purpose of such circles tends to be on quality improvement rather than cost reduction, the best-run Quality Circles emphasize both.

Where there are no such meetings currently in place, the company could develop regular interaction of employees both inside and outside the relevant departments to discuss cost savings.

With the active involvement of employees from the officer level down, the company can continuously identify opportunities for cost improvement. But it isn't enough to discuss such opportunities. For best results, the company should formalize a system for monitoring cost-control opportunities as they are identified and ensure that they are implemented.

Use cost-reduction tools periodically to conduct a review of individual departments and units.

Periodically, each company officer and manager should be responsible for conducting a comprehensive review of the activities performed by his or her organization, using the tools and mechanisms for cost reduction as a base. Functional analysis, requirements analysis, reengineering, cost analysis, and organizational analysis—all discussed in detail in the first section of this book—should be applied every few years on a department-by-department basis to determine whether there are opportunities for improvement within each department. There usually are.

Even the best managers could stand to perform a comprehensive review of what they are doing and involve outsiders in the process. If the organization staggers these reviews, so that only a few departments are reviewed each year, the impact on the total organization can be minimized. And when combined with an effective cost-control program, the results will not be as dramatic or affect the work force as drastically as a review of the entire organization.

Promises and intentions are fine, but get it in writing.

When ideas to control costs are developed, they should be provided in writing. The form used varies by company, but generally contains the following elements:

IDEA	Combine the purchasing and warehousing departments in the field offices
POTENTIAL SAVINGS	$200,000 per year
COSTS	One-time $15,000 charge for computer system changes
DATE TO BE COMPLETED	July 1, 1998
REMARKS	The consolidated field office location will have to be ready by the end of 1997. The vacated warehouses and offices can be rented out fairly easily in the current market. There will be some minor delays in providing materials to certain remote locations, but that will not create significant delays in meeting customer requirements.

Complex ideas and suggestions may require additional detail, such as the interim steps required before the suggestion can be implemented or special interest groups (such as regulators or union leaders) that should be contacted before the company proceeds with the suggestion.

Company managers and officers should be responsible for developing suggestions regularly for cost improvements such as these, and after discussion with the relevant user groups, implementing those improvements. The chief executive officer can use these written summaries to track promised completion dates against actual progress and to track cost savings promised against those actually achieved.

There should also be an effort to recast the budget for major cost-reduction ideas. As in the above example, to consolidate certain purchasing and warehousing facilities, the 1999 budgets for those functions should be reduced by the $200,000 annual savings projected for this cost-saving idea. In 1998, the budgets should be reduced by only $100,000, because the idea is projected to be implemented on July 1, 1998, and therefore only one half of a full year's savings will be achieved.

It will be difficult, of course, to recast budgets constantly every time a new cost-saving suggestion is implemented. Accordingly, in the first year in which such an idea is implemented, the company may prefer to examine the budget-vs.-actual statements manually to verify that expenses are running less than budgeted, and that the difference is due to this cost-reduction program. In the next full year of the implementation of this idea, the full cost savings can be reflected during the routine annual budgeting process.

Many successful ideas can be developed by requiring managers and officers to continually examine their own operations, and those of others, to determine new and less costly ways of performing their functions. More reductions can be obtained by showing managers the actual cost of the services they use.

> Corporate services are like campaign pamphlets: Giving them away is relatively easy, but selling them is nearly impossible.

Of the hundreds of departments I have reviewed, my award for "Most Picked-On Department In Any Organization" is: Information Systems.

In almost every type of business organization, the Information Systems department is the butt of much criticism: "They don't do systems development or maintenance fast enough. They go too fast and leave confused potential users in their dust. They aren't up-to-date on the latest technology, allowing our competitors to get ahead of us. They're addicted to the latest technology, and IBM knows it, so IBM has us in their hip pocket. Everyone in this company has a personal computer, whether they need it or not, because Information Systems says they have to have one. No one in this company gets personal computers, because Information Systems doesn't like them." In one instance, all of these seemingly contradictory criticisms came from different people within the same company!

This high level of criticism comes for a number of reasons. Good information systems are a tremendous competitive advantage for most companies. (Some types of companies, such as airlines, live or die by the quality of their information systems.)

Rapid progress in computer technology also leaves many company employees feeling confused and somewhat helpless, and they sometimes feel overly dependent on the Information Systems department for support. Still other employees, who play games on their personal computers in the evenings, feel like experts in the subject of computer operations and constantly second-guess the decisions of their computer specialists.

But one factor also contributes greatly to the high level of comment and concern about information systems: In most companies, computer development and information systems support are free services, provided to almost all employees without charge. When you call your information systems department for help or support for your personal computer, or to develop or maintain a system, does the cost of that help show up on your budget? In some companies it does. In companies where it doesn't, however, the demand for the services of information systems intensifies. And so does the frustration with the quality and timeliness of those services, as the Information Systems department struggles to be responsive to virtually all of the organization's employees.

Many companies, therefore, have developed "charge-back systems" for such services. Under such a system, the Information Systems Department has no budget. Instead, each user department is charged, in its own budget, for services performed for that department by Information Systems. The head of the information systems group must then "sell" the services of that department to others within the corporation, just as those others must market the company's services to its customers. And, like other customers, the company's managers are free to seek other suppliers.

At one company, the cost of janitorial and custodial services were allocated to each department at the company. Appalled at the ever-increasing charge for such services that routinely appeared on their budgets, the company managers looked at contracting out the custodial services. After they found a cleaning service that would do the work for substantially less cost, the managers approached their senior executives who agreed to contract out the work, which resulted in significant cost savings.

Interestingly, this approach avoided one of the problems common with cost-reduction ideas. If no chargeback system had been in place at this company, and if senior management had simply ordered the managers to deal with a cleaning service instead of full-time janitors and custodians, the managers would almost certainly have complained about the quality of cleaning provided by the cleaning service, the timeliness and appearance of the work crews, the inability to reach the cleaning service during normal business hours, and anything else they could think of.

However, because the managers themselves had come up with this idea, they worked to correct problems as they occurred. Their vested interest in the idea committed them to make it work.

A chargeback system is different from an "overhead allocation" system. Under overhead allocation, the company charges a straight percentage or dollar amount to all departments, using a predetermined formula. There is little that an individual department can do to change its overhead allocation amount.

On the other hand, a chargeback system involves charging user departments for services as they are rendered, on a dollar-per-hour or other payment mechanism. An individual department can then reduce those costs by reducing its use of those corporate services or by contracting with outsiders to perform that service at a lower cost.

Some of the corporate services that can be subject to a chargeback system include:

- *Legal services,* including litigation support as well as routine review of legal documents

- *Accounting and financial services,* such as economic analysis and projections for specific projects or tax accounting for selected departments or units

- *Building and custodial services,* including building maintenance as well as janitorial services

- *Information systems,* including development of new systems as well as system maintenance and support

- *Engineering,* particularly engineering related to a specific project or function

- *Construction and maintenance,* particularly where construction and maintenance are related to specific projects within the organization

This should not be considered as an exclusive list, of course. Virtually everything that the organization does for itself can be charged back.

Think back to our earlier discussion of services that directly benefit the customer versus services that indirectly benefit the customer. Most of the services that indirectly benefit the customer should be charged back internally to departments or units within the organization, while services that directly benefit the customer should be charged directly to the customer.

"Unbundling" was a popular term during the deregulatory heyday of the 1980s. In a regulatory sense, unbundling referred to the separating of services traditionally provided to customers as a unit in order to allow the customer to shop around for each individual service and get the lowest price for each. For example, telephone companies separated out (or "unbundled") long-distance and local services, allowing customers to choose among alternative long-distance carriers.

Chargeback systems allow for a corporate unbundling of services. These systems allow your managers and executives to shop around for each service provided by your organization, which not only encourages them to find the lowest priced alternative for each, but also provides an incentive to the supplying departments to operate as cheaply as possible.

As with most forms of major corporate overhaul, the institution of a chargeback system will not initially be popular with many of your employees. It requires strange new paperwork, unfamiliar budgeting processes, and—perhaps most frightening—it forces managers who haven't had to sell their services in decades to get out into their market and strut their stuff. It's a traumatic psychological change, particularly for those departments that provide the administrative and corporate services being charged back.

When the chargeback system becomes more familiar to your employees, however, the resistance will tend to fade. Your best employees will rise to the challenge, and—both from within and outside the administrative and corporate services departments—will find innovative new ways to perform functions for the company. Their reward will come in the form of improved budget performance and profitability for their units.

As your managers and executives continually look for ways to improve the cost-effectiveness of the organization, the lower-level employees will begin to understand the importance of cost effectiveness in the grand design of the company. The best employees will want to participate in the process and should be encouraged to do so. The fundamental human resource systems in the company—including hiring, promoting, compensation, and communications— should be geared toward making such participation possible and toward recognizing and rewarding the efforts of your employees in reducing your costs and improving the bottom line for your company.

12

Compensation and Communication (How Can the Entire Organization Get Involved in Cost Control?)

> Your employees are your biggest and most important investment. Make sure that they are properly leveraged.

One electric utility had a problem with its meter readers. They simply weren't working fast enough, and it was costing the company big money.

Meter reading is an expensive, labor-intensive activity at most utilities. Typically, meter readers trudge from one house to another reading meters to determine their usage of electricity and gas. Obviously, the quicker the meter readers work, the less cost there is per meter, and the more successful the utility is at meeting the needs of its customers.

Unfortunately, at this utility the productivity of the meter readers was way below the accepted industry averages. When we talked to some of the meter readers, we found out why.

"The boss tells us how many meters to read per day," one meter reader told us. What happens if they don't get all their meters read in one day, we asked. "Then we read them the next day," was the reply. In other words, no incentive for fast work and no penalty for slow.

When we asked their supervisor how he determined the number of meters to be read by each meter reader, the answer was: "I base it on the number of meters that the person has been able to read in the past." Aha! The slower a meter reader worked, the lower the expectations of that employee for the future. No wonder the meter readers were trying to outdo each other in slowness.

We tested the system by promising confidentiality and then asking one meter reader, who then averaged 250 to 300 meters per day, how many he could read per day if the company paid him fifty cents for each meter correctly read. "Confidentially?" he asked. Yes, we promised; we wouldn't tell his boss and he wouldn't get in trouble for his answer. He didn't hesitate in his response. "Seven hundred."

Compensation is a critical component in a successful cost-control program, and it means more than just salary and benefits. It means recognition and non-monetary compensation as well.

Some utilities have successfully improved their productivity and provided their meter readers with additional compensation without costing their customers an additional penny. Where their meter readers were typically reading at a rate of about 350 meters per day, one company upped that quota to a seemingly-impossible 500 meters per day—with the added incentive that, after all meters had been read and verified, the meter readers were finished for the day. Readers who finished at 2:00 or 3:00 in the afternoon could head home and not have to wait around or find more meters to read until the traditional closing hour of 4:30 p.m. The result: The average read rate quickly climbed to 500 meters per day.

Naturally, this productivity enhancement also had to be accompanied by some quality-control mechanisms. When meter readers were informed that they could go home after all meters were read, there was a tendency—in their haste—to become somewhat sloppy in entering the meter data. Perhaps worse, some readers hurried through their routes, tromping on flower beds, vaulting over backyard fences, pushing obstacles out of their way and into driveways, sidewalks, and streets.

After a few customer complaints about incorrect bills and dead flowers, the company provided extensive training in customer relations to the meter readers. This was coupled with a quality-control program where the right to go home early hinged not only upon the number of meters read but on the number of meters that were read correctly, and the number of customer complaints about the reader's work habits. An unacceptable number of incorrect reads or customer complaints caused some meter readers to stay behind and be retrained, while others went home.

And, of course, productivity quickly settled in at the expected 500-per-day standard set by the company, with virtually no incentive to do better. The supervisors constantly had to walk the meter-reading routes themselves and adjust standards to reflect new construction and more experience among the meter-reading personnel. In other words, supervisors had to become more active in their day-to-day management of the work of subordinates.

Once the new procedures were established, however, meter readers became more productive. Consequently, when older meter readers retired or resigned, the company could afford not to replace those workers. And the concept of employee reduction through attrition goes over far better—with customers, regulators, board members, as well as employees—than wholesale layoffs or reductions in staff.

To involve the entire organization in the development and implementation of cost-control programs on an ongoing basis, the organization should:

- Communicate to all employees, not only regarding the need for effective cost control, but also the targets that each employee is expected to achieve for cost improvement

- Compensate employees in a way that rewards cost control and cost reduction, and penalizes attempts to overspend.

But this is easier said than done. Particularly in large companies it involves a tremendous communications effort and a radical change in systems with which your employees have become comfortable.

> Your employees should share the risk—and the rewards—of your business.

In the world of finance, "leverage" refers to the degree to which the business reaps the rewards of its success. A highly leveraged company is one whose equity is composed primarily of debt rather than stock. When the company's earned rate of return exceeds the interest rate on its debt, the stockholders make a fortune. When the earned rate of return is less than the interest rate . . . well, that better not happen for too long.

You can leverage your employees the same way that you leverage the financial structure of your company. Let's structure each employee's compensation on the following formula:

$$A + (B \times C) = D$$

In this formula, "D" represents total cash compensation, or the amount of money that you would expect the employee to earn in a normal business year. "A" represents base salary, which is the amount that the employee requires to "survive"; that is, to pay for food, clothing, and housing expenses plus enough for day-to-day living. "B" represents incentive compensation. It is the additional amount that you would pay your employee for the results he or she achieved during the year.

That leaves us with C, which, unfortunately, requires another formula:

$$C = \frac{\text{(The economic performance your company actually had)}}{\text{(The economic performance projected for your company)}}$$

If the company had twice as good a year as it expected to have, as calculated from the targets developed in its strategic plan, each employee's incentive compensation would be twice as large as expected. If the company didn't make any money, no incentive compensation would be paid. (If the company lost money, then "C" would equal zero. No point in making it negative; it would be difficult to get your employees to write a check to cover your company's loss.)

Does your company have this type of incentive compensation system already? You may think it does. I'll bet it doesn't.

Many profit-making institutions have some form of what they call "incentive compensation," and even some nonprofit institutions are incorporating an incentive structure into their wage and salary systems. But in too many cases, incentive compensation simply translates into either (1) an agreement with the employee to pay an amount to be determined arbitrarily by the company at the end of the year based on an unknown and uncommunicated formula, or (2) a predetermined amount set by the company at the beginning of the year and paid almost irrespective of actual performance (also known as the "I already know what my bonus is going to be" syndrome.)

If your company has an incentive compensation system, consider the following questions:

- Does the incentive compensation apply to virtually everyone in the company, and not just to managers and executives?

- Does everyone understand the basis on which the incentive compensation is paid?

- Is the incentive compensation paid both on overall company performance as well as individual performance?

- To the extent that incentive compensation is based on overall company performance, is routine information provided to employees that shows how the company is doing against its target?

- To the extent that incentive compensation is based on individual performance, are the specific goals and targets—and the financial implications of hitting, missing, or exceeding those targets—clearly explained to and understood by each employee?

- Do the targets for individual employees include targets for controlling and reducing costs?

- When the incentive compensation checks are handed out, is the link between the amount paid and performance of the company and the individual relative to the predetermined targets clearly documented and communicated?

The answer to each question should be yes. At far too many companies, the answer to most of the questions is no.

Remember, from our discussion of the strategic planning and budgeting process, that we developed targets for the company, departments, and individuals. The individual targets can be translated into individual targets with incentive compensation implications by using a worksheet such as this at the beginning of each year:

American Ice and Candle Company GOALS FOR THE COMING YEAR	
GOAL	WEIGHTING
To sell 500 blocks of ice	65%
To sell 400 candles	25%
To operate within or below budget	10%
TOTAL (MUST EQUAL 100%)	100%
TARGET BONUS	$10,000 (To be adjusted based on company performance)

This tells the employee several things. If he or she performs on target, and if the company performs as projected, the expected bonus is $10,000. And the employee should concentrate on selling ice, which accounts for 65 percent of the total bonus.

It may be helpful to provide a range for each goal as well. For example, the company may set 500 blocks of ice as the standard to be met, with a minimum of 0 blocks sold (for which no bonus would be paid) to a maximum of 1000 blocks (where, if the employee met or exceeded that sales figure, the weighting would be doubled).

At the end of the year, the goals worksheet would be completed as follows:

American Ice and Candle Company			
GOALS VS. ACTUAL PERFORMANCE FOR THE PAST YEAR			
GOAL	INITIAL WEIGHT	ACTUAL PERFORMANCE	FINAL WEIGHT
To sell 500 blocks of ice	65	567 blocks of ice sold	74
To sell 400 candles	25	362 candles sold	22
To operate within or below budget	10	Came in on budget	10
TOTALS	100		106

For goals and objectives that lend themselves to quantitative analysis such as these, final weights can be calculated using a formula such as this:

$$\text{Final weight} = \frac{\text{Actual performance}}{\text{Target performance}} \times \text{Original weight}$$

For example, this employee concentrated on the most heavily weighted goal, which was selling blocks of ice. The original target was 500 blocks of ice, and 567 were sold; 567 divided by 500 is 1.134, so this employee's performance exceeded expectations by 13.4 percent. If we increase the original 65 weighting by 13.4 percent, the new weighting is 74. Similarly, if we reduce the weighting to reflect the fact that the employee's sales quota for candles was missed, the weighting for that factor declines by three points.

Not all goals lend themselves nicely to mathematical equations such as these, of course. Although goals should be as qualitative as possible, there may be some that will be a matter of judgment. And even among quantitative goals, not all will be as nicely linear as the above examples. For example, a colder than normal summer may impact the market for ice blocks far beyond the capacity of any individual salesperson to overcome.

In any event, our hypothetical employee has outperformed targets by six percent and is entitled to a bonus of 106 percent of $10,000, or $10,600. That figure must now be adjusted for overall company performance. After all, if the company doesn't have any money, bonuses can't be paid—regardless of how well an individual employee did.

Fortunately, the American Ice and Candle Company greatly outperformed expectations. Specifically, the company did twice as well as originally projected. Accordingly, the company may double our employee's bonus to $21,200. Chances are, however, that there will not be quite so direct a correlation between how well the company did and how much the bonus will be adjusted. After all, if the company did so much better than projected, it's likely that a large number of individual employees exceeded their individual targets also. Therefore, some of the company's success may be reflected in the individually weighted bonuses.

A number of sensitivity analyses should be performed at the beginning of the year to give managers and employees a rough idea of how overall company performance would translate into individual bonuses. One company provided each employee with the following chart at the beginning of the year:

Earnings	$10 million	$20 million	$30 million	$40 million
Bonus Factor	0.5	1.0	1.5	2.0

At the end of that year, each employee would get a preliminary bonus figure calculated on his or her own personal performance against the targets established at the beginning of the year. That preliminary bonus would then be multiplied by the "bonus factor" shown above, which was based on the earnings for the year. Thus, if the company earned $10 million that year, each bonus would be multiplied by 0.5—essentially cutting each bonus in half. On the other hand, earnings of $40 million would result in each individual bonus being doubled.

When each employee in the company receives a bonus that is clearly tied both to individual and companywide performance, cost-effectiveness suddenly becomes a critical issue that ripples throughout the work force.

> To the maximum possible extent, each employee should be responsible for generating his or her own "profit."

So far, we've discussed two bases for incentive compensation: overall company performance, and individual performance. A third is also appropriate where feasible: "unit" or "departmental" incentives.

Under this structure, each department in the organization is considered to be part of a profit center. For example, the manufacturing unit in the company "sells" its product to the marketing group, which then sells it to customers at a hypothetical "markup." Sales prices multiplied by the number of units sold equals revenue. Costs are subtracted from the revenue, and the profit for the department or unit is calculated.

How are internal prices for goods and services calculated? The issue of transfer pricing is one that has fascinated and confounded economists and accountants for decades, but some options include:

• Using the wholesale price in the market as a guide when the product or service is provided at wholesale by other companies.

- Breaking down the product or service into its component parts if there is no reliable market guide to its wholesale price. For example, one company made a unique product that could not be readily compared to any other product. But by determining the wholesale price of each of the component parts, the company developed a workable basis for its internal transfer price

- Using historical cost accounting data to calculate the cost of the goods manufactured, then adding a negotiated reasonable profit margin. Often, the profit margin on the product or service—the difference between the price received by the customer and the cost of manufacturing the product—is simply split evenly among the manufacturing and distribution departments within the company.

What about the administrative functions, such as the legal or accounting departments? Recall our earlier discussion about chargeback systems, where most of these departments would not have budgets of their own. These departments would be responsible essentially for selling its services to other units or departments within the company.

Many of these departments—including such functions as legal services, accounting, advertising, information systems, building maintenance, and medical services—could operate in an internal free market. They could charge whatever price they wanted to the other departments in the company, with the understanding that those other departments could either (1) reduce their demand for those services, or (2) look to outside law firms, advertising agencies, or clinics to meet their needs.

This lesson was brought home at one large consulting firm. This firm offered not only routine management consulting services, but other specialized services such as public relations and marketing. One vice president in the management consulting division had recently taken on a huge project for a major client. The project required, among other things, significant marketing and communications support. Accordingly, the vice president in charge of this project approached the head of the marketing and communications unit with the requirements for the project.

The marketing and communications person listened and nodded as the VP described the project and the communications needs. Then the VP asked what it would cost the client to get the communications support that was required.

"I don't know," the marketing person said.

"Well, could you give me a rough idea?" the VP asked.

"No," was the reply, "we don't work that way. But we'll start doing the work for you, and we'll just bill your client for whatever work we do." When the VP protested this cavalier approach to project management, the marketing person appeared shocked. "What do you care? The client is paying for it, not you."

Somewhat disgusted with the performance of his own organization, the VP subsequently called several outside advertising and public relations firms, describing the requirements of this assignment. Before the day was over, he found one that listened carefully, gave a reasonable written estimate, and had a good reputation with previous clients. And on that basis, the VP gave the work to an outside advertising firm, choosing them over another department within his own firm.

Controversial? You bet. Several high-level officers in the consulting firm accused the VP of not being a "team player." But others in the company were supportive of the VP's action. And the VP's clients appreciated the product that he and his crew provided. On the other hand, those who were "team players" in the consulting firm and allowed the marketing and advertising unit to gouge their clients, soon found themselves with no clients to gouge.

Companies that are organized into profit centers have the greatest potential for ongoing cost control on the part of all employees. It is difficult to comprehend how reducing the number of paper clips and reams of paper used at the copying machine will affect the bottom line of a large company, but it is far easier to understand how small money-saving steps will improve the profitability of a department or unit within that company.

There are several ways that departmental profitability can be factored into an incentive compensation program.

One way is to add it as another factor to be considered by the company in developing the incentive compensation for each individual within the department:

American Ice and Candle Company GOALS VS. ACTUAL PERFORMANCE FOR THE PAST YEAR			
GOAL	INITIAL WEIGHT	ACTUAL PERFORMANCE	FINAL WEIGHT
To sell five hundred blocks of ice	60	567 blocks of ice sold	73
To sell four hundred candles	20	362 candles sold	18
To operate within or below expense budget	5	Came in on budget	5
TO OPERATE THE UNIT AT A 20 PERCENT MARGIN	15	OPERATED AT A 30 PERCENT MARGIN	23
TOTALS	100		119

Another method is to make an overall adjustment for departmental profitability, rather than corporate profitability. But that is recommended only where departments are clearly and obviously self-contained businesses on their own.

When everyone in the company understands the importance of cost control and improved margins, and particularly when the results are linked to compensation for each employee, the entire company will work toward improved cost-effectiveness.

> There's no law that says you have to pay your employees the same amount of money every month.

The more that compensation is adjusted to reflect company performance, the more sensitive your employees will be to improving company performance. The reason that bonuses are paid annually is because employees like to have a lump sum paid to them once a year, as a kind of forced savings. However, it is also partly due to administrative simplicity.

With information systems technology becoming increasingly advanced, it may be possible to calculate progress against the strategic plan and individual goals on a quarterly, monthly, or more frequent basis, and provide at least a part of the incentive compensation to employees on an ongoing basis. In this manner, paycheck amounts would vary somewhat from month to month or week to week, and employees would receive tangible financial evidence of the company's financial performance in every paycheck. This may be beyond the realm of technology for many companies, but won't be soon.

In any event, there are several other ways to compensate employees in ways other than a straight monthly salary:

- Where appropriate, pay employees on a piecemeal basis. If employees in a given unit are required to produce a certain amount of a given product, why not pay them by the unit? If you are running a hotel, consider paying the maids a set amount for each room cleaned, rather than giving them a straight salary regardless of the number of rooms they've serviced. The advantages: greater customer responsiveness (because more rooms will be ready for more customers on a more timely basis) and more cost-effectiveness (if maids operate more productively, fewer maids are required, thus reducing benefits and administrative costs related to employment).

- Alternatively, consider letting employees go home when the work is done. When this is accompanied by production quotas that exceed the current level of production, your employees will often surprise you by exceeding the highest levels of productivity ever achieved. As a result, your costs go down—and morale actually goes up!

The downside to such compensation mechanisms is that quality may be sacrificed to quantity, as employees rush to produce as much as possible to make as much money as they can, or as they hurry to get home to watch their favorite television rerun. Accordingly, the supervisors and managers of such employees should have strict quality control goals as part of their own incentive compensation, measured by customer satisfaction surveys and inspections of finished work.

Above all, communicate.

Communication is by far the most important element in a successful program of cost control. If you want to reduce costs and keep a handle on expenses, tell your employees . . . and tell them . . . and tell them.

When we've conducted cost-reduction studies, absolutely the best clients—the ones that were most interested in the project and the ones most willing to roll up their sleeves and do the painful and difficult work involved in successful cost reduction—were those where the need to reduce costs was explained and clearly understood throughout the company.

One such company had been running huge losses for several years, and the company's management made no secret to its employees about the eminent dangers that lurked if their losses continued. The employees buckled down and concentrated on reducing costs. As a result, their expenses were reduced by about 20 percent. Four years later, during a major recession, they were in such robust financial health that they became a "white knight" for other troubled companies in their area as they began an active program of acquiring other similar businesses—at bargain basement prices.

On the other hand, another company pursued a radically different course. Although business was down, as a privately held consulting firm it didn't feel compelled to share its increasingly disappointing financial results with all of its employees. Even worse, the company disguised its financial condition from its employees by struggling to keep incentive compensation payments as high as possible.

Employees could only speculate on the financial condition of the company based upon clues and rumors. Productivity dropped drastically as employees became distracted with trying to read the tea leaves to determine the economic condition of the company. Morale plummeted. The company's management eventually slashed randomly at the work force with one round of layoffs after another.

You can effectively communicate with your employees by developing and distributing a strategic plan and budget, linking that plan and budget to an incentive compensation program, encouraging managers and employees to prune costs—while continually reinforcing these programs through publications, meetings, video tape presentations, or other media.

Above all, honesty pays dividends. If things aren't going well, your employees should know as early as possible. They should know it from the presentations you make, the memos you circulate—and the bonuses they no longer earn. They'll help you get the organization back on its feet.

Your employees want your company to succeed. Their own financial happiness depends upon it. They are a resource that you can draw upon if you choose honestly to share your historical track record, goals, and objectives with them.

Communicate.

13

What Happens After Cost Control?

Cost control never ends.

When you implement your cost-control mechanisms, the initial reaction of your employees will be: When will this be over? It may take years before they finally get the message. It's *never* over.

It was probably the same with the company, centuries ago, that first decided to put together a written budget. As the early clerks struggled with an abacus or quill pens to figure out what their future expenses would be, they probably were of one thought: "This is keeping me away from my *real* work."

Cost control is part of the "real work" of the organization. Don't misunderstand. Like preparing a budget, it's not the most important thing that your organization does. You can't "cost cut" your way to success. In order to succeed, you have to develop a strategy that is responsive to the market, develop a high quality product or service, actively market and promote that service, and stay in touch continuously with your customers and your competitors to determine what is going on in your market. If you are highly successful, your company is the one that is driving the market. Virtually none of that has anything to do with cost control.

Cost control is a supplement to those activities and represents a way to differentiate yourself among your competitors in the market for:

- Your product or service, because your cost will be lower than your competition

- Stock or debt, because your expenses will be lower than your competition

- High quality employees, because your employment record will be more stable than that of your competition.

By continually examining the functions your organization performs and reassessing them to determine whether they are necessary, your company will avoid the mistakes that your competition will make by implementing across-the-board cost cuts during economic crunch times, then restaffing at even higher levels later—thus whipsawing the company through the good and bad times.

Successful cost control requires an understanding on the part of all employees that it isn't just another fad being followed by the company's management. And there is only one thing that will convince employees of that: Time.

When that company, years ago, took steps to develop the first written budgets in business history, its employees almost certainly spent the end of each year hoping that their management would forget to send the papers around for the next year's budget exercise. When the papers did come around, you can bet that there was plenty of moaning and complaining around the coffee maker . . . or at the aqueduct . . . or during intermission at the gladiator tournaments . . . or whatever.

Nobody likes preparing budgets, and nobody is going to like developing goals and objectives with specific performance targets, keying those goals and objectives to budget dollars, constantly re-examining their own activities and pruning those that are unnecessary, and continuously exhorting employees to keep costs down.

But everybody likes employment stability, increased compensation, and market recognition for a high-value, low-cost product. And while a successful cost-control program alone cannot make any such guarantees, the establishment of such a program is a necessary component to achieve those results.

Like everything else in business, cost control isn't a quick fix. It's a long haul with benefits that often come slowly. But where all employees understand that the organization must operate as cost-effectively as possible and work continuously to develop new ways to do precisely that, the company—and its employees—will prosper.

Appendix

Do You Have a Cost-Effective Organization?

Taking this quiz isn't as good as hiring a consultant.
But this quiz won't charge you $350 an hour, either.

This final section provides a check list that you can use to determine whether your organization is operating cost-effectively in all of its activities. Although this check list is by no means complete, it does provide a starting point to determine what types of opportunities exist for improvement in your company.

If you are interested in looking at this check list as a "quiz" for your company, each question is weighted for its importance to the cost-effectiveness of your organization. Give your company a full or partial score, depending upon what you think it deserves. For example, the first question, "Is a strategic plan in place for your organization?" is worth a total of 10 points. If there is no such plan anywhere, the company earns no points. If there is a formal, well-documented, well-understood plan, the company earns all 10 points. If there is something of a plan in place, but it is not sufficiently formal or complete, give the strategic plan somewhere between 0 and 10 points, depending upon your opinion of its completeness and usefulness.

A scale upon which to gauge the results is provided at the conclusion of this check list.

PART A: CORPORATE COST-CONTROL SYSTEMS

This section looks at the "big picture." Here, we identify the broad programs and procedures that are in place to facilitate cost control in your organization.

- Is there a strategic plan in place for your organization? (10 points)

- Is the strategic plan well-communicated and understood by all employees? (10 points)

- Is the strategic plan linked to the operating and capital budget so that each dollar spent by the company is linked to a corporate goal or objective? (10 points)

- Is the strategic plan linked to the performance appraisal and compensation system so that each person's performance relative to the strategic plan is recognized and, where appropriate, rewarded? (10 points)

- Is "cost effectiveness" built into the strategic plan as a goal to be achieved by the organization? (10 points)

- With regard to the organization structure:

  - Are the number of layers in the organization appropriate? (10 points)

  - Are the "spans of control" (the number of people reporting to each manager) sufficient to keep each manager busy? (10 points)

- Is the budget developed by your company easy to understand and follow, and does it yield sufficient information for the management and day-to-day operation of your organization? (10 points)

- Is a variance report (a report that compares the budget to actual cost data throughout the course of the year) circulated throughout your company on a timely basis? Is it easy to understand, and does it provide sufficient information for you to make adjustments to your spending throughout the year? (10 points)

- Does your company penalize managers who go over budget on expenses, and reward those who stay at or below budget? (10 points)

- Is there a chargeback system in place for administrative functions such as information systems, so that those functions are billed directly to those departments that use them? If so, does that system work effectively? (10 points)

- Does your company communicate the need to control expenses throughout the organization? Does it reward those who do control expenses, and follow up on recommendations and ideas to reduce costs from employees below the level of manager? (20 points)

- Are your profits generally higher than those of your competition? (60 points)

- Are your costs generally lower than those of your competition? (60 points)

PART B: INDIVIDUAL COST-CONTROL INITIATIVES

While by no means a complete list, this next section probes some individual steps that a cost-effective organization might take to keep costs down in representative departments or units. These questions were selected because they are generic and apply to most organizations; however, it is possible that not all of them will apply to your organization.

ACCOUNTING/FINANCE

- Are the reports generated by the accounting and finance departments all necessary to the management and operations of your company? (3 points)

- Are bills sent out to customers on a timely basis? (2 points)

- Are steps taken to quickly follow up on and resolve delinquent payments? (2 points)

- When checks are received from customers, are they deposited quickly and the funds invested immediately? (3 points)

- Are the accounting and financial functions in your company appropriately computerized? (3 points)

- Has the company considered contracting out—or bringing in-house—all or some of the accounting functions, such as payroll? (3 points)

PUBLIC/GOVERNMENT RELATIONS

- Are the publications that you provide to customers, employees, retirees, stockholders, and the general public all periodically reviewed to determine whether their distribution (in terms of number of people and frequency) is necessary and appropriate? (2 points)

- Do the public and government relations departments draw appropriately upon employees at other departments for assistance in lobbying or public service activities? (Some public and government relations departments reserve these activities entirely for themselves—despite the fact that many employees in other departments may enjoy participating in these activities—and overstaff as a result.) (1 point)

LEGAL

- Has your company recently reviewed its legal services to determine whether outside legal services could be brought in-house; or, alternatively, whether work done in-house could be done more effectively outside? (2 points)

- Does your company make appropriate use of paralegals for routine research and drafting of legal documents? (1 point)

- Is the secretarial support in your legal department staffed appropriately? (Many legal departments staff their clerical support for peak loads to allow for last-minute filing deadlines in courts and regulatory agencies. The clerical staff should, instead, be staffed for the "base" or normal load, with the legal department drawing upon other departments for secretarial support in a crunch.) (1 point)

INFORMATION SYSTEMS

- Has the company recently reviewed its information systems services to determine whether some or all of those services could be contracted out; or, alternatively, whether work done by contractors could be brought in-house less expensively? (2 points)

- After a new computer system is developed, is there a good system in place to follow-up and ensure that the cost savings promised for that system are achieved? (3 points)

PROCUREMENT/PURCHASING/WAREHOUSING

- Are inventories kept reasonably low? (2 points)

- Does the company keep reasonable control of purchases? (In some companies, a substantial number of purchases are made "off line," bypassing the normal procurement process and thereby preventing the company from taking full advantage of quantity discounts or inventory management.) (2 points)

- Has your company minimized (or better yet, eliminated) the amount of paper required to execute purchase orders? (2 points)

- Does the company ensure that bids are solicited from several vendors wherever possible? (2 points)

CORPORATE/ADMINISTRATIVE SERVICES

- Has the company recently reviewed administrative services such as building maintenance, custodial and janitorial services, vehicle maintenance, and printing services to determine whether those services are being appropriately performed either in-house or by an outside contractor? (2 points)

- Has the company minimized (or better yet, eliminated) the amount of paper required for records storage and retrieval? (1 point)

- Are the number of cars and other vehicles provided to company employees reasonable? (1 point)

HUMAN RESOURCES

- Does the company continually monitor the levels of overtime and the number of dollars spent on contractors, to determine whether the organization could save money by adding additional staff? (3 points)

- Are training functions sufficiently coordinated, thus avoiding duplication? (1 point)

- Has the company examined the benefits of contracting out benefits design and administration functions as opposed to performing them in-house? (1 point)

CUSTOMER SERVICE

- Is the productivity of both telephone and in-person customer representatives carefully tracked and monitored? (2 points)

- Does the company periodically review any field offices to ensure that they all are necessary and cost justified? (3 points)

To determine the steps that your company needs to take to maintain or improve its cost-effectiveness, provide the following information:

1. What was your score on Part A?
   (out of 250 total points)   _____

2. What was your total *possible* score
   on Part B (there were 50 total points,
   but not all of the questions may have
   been relevant to your organization)?   _____

3. What was the score you *actually*
    received on Part B?   _____

4. Divide the score you actually received
    on Part B (item 3 above) by the total
    possible score (item 2)   _____

Item 1 above now represents your score on Part A, and
Item 4 represents your score on Part B.

Gauge your score based upon the matrix shown on the
following chart. Recognize, of course, that without an
extensive review of all of the functions performed by an
organization, this survey can only provide a preliminary
observation regarding your business and its operations.
Nonetheless, this check list and survey can provide an important first step toward recognizing and overcoming the
barriers that your company faces in becoming cost-effective, and in meeting the challenges of your increasingly
cost-effective competition.

| | | SCORE ON PART A
Corporate Cost-Control Initiatives | |
		Low (125 or less)	High (More than 125)
SCORE ON PART B Individual Cost-Control Initiatives	High (More than 0.5)	This company appears to be pursuing initiatives on an individual or departmental basis but hasn't fully developed cost-effectiveness as a recognized goal of the organization. The company should concentrate on developing cost-control mechanisms such as strategic planning and budgeting while continuing to encourage its employees to pursue the initiatives they have taken.	This company is most likely to be functioning in a cost-effective manner. The company should continue encouraging cost control for all managers and employees, conducting a thorough cost-reduction effort primarily where selected departments or activities appear ineffective.
	Low (0.5 or less)	It is likely that this company has a long road to travel in order to become cost-effective. The company should start with a complete cost-reduction review, examining all of its functions in a comprehensive manner. Then it should develop overall cost-control mechanisms to ensure that the company doesn't backslide into its old culture.	A link is missing from this company's chain. Most of the mechanisms are in place to monitor costs, but the word just isn't filtering down into the ranks. The company should conduct a comprehensive cost-reduction effort, actively involving all employees. Then communicate the need for continued cost reduction on an ongoing basis throughout the organization.

Index